Developing an Electron Edge

Adam Lynch and Max Gfeller

Developing an Electron Edge

ISBN 978-1-939902-39-9
Published by: Bleeding Edge Press, Santa Rosa, CA 95404
Title: Developing an Electron Edge
Authors: Adam Lynch and Max Gfeller
Acquisitions Editor: Christina Rudloff
Editor: Troy Mott
Copy Editor: Christina Rudloff and Troy Mott
Cover Art: Martin Murtonen
Website: bleedingedgepress.com

Table of Contents

Preface

Why use Electron?

Electron combines Chromium and Node.js, empowering you to create real desktop apps with HTML, CSS, and JavaScript, which integrate tightly into the desktop environment. In **Developing an Electron Edge**, we cover all things Electron. We have used Electron 1.1.0 for this book. We breakdown what Electron is and what you can achieve with it over a typical desktop or Web app. Not only will we cover the complete development process from beginning to end, but the packaging and delivery of your app as well. You'll discover some platform specific issues, learn how to deploy automatic updates, and even take a look at using one code base for the desktop and the Web.

Who this book is for

Developing an Electron Edge is for anyone looking to keep up with the cutting edge of desktop application development. If you have ever wanted to create a cross-platform desktop app and put your Web app on users' desktops, you will love this book. If you're a Web developer or a Node.js user, you'll be pleasantly surprised by how easy it is, given how your existing skills will be leveraged throughout. Newcomers are introduced to the power of Electron, Web technologies, and Node.js, although we do assume you have some JavaScript literacy. Don't worry if you've been around the block, or if you already use Electron. We go into plenty of detail on some of the more advanced topics or obstacles you'll face in order to deliver a rich desktop app. This book is full of potential pitfalls and lessons learned from real world experience, as well as covering intricate subjects like distributing your app to end users. There is something in this book for everyone.

What this book is about

Chapter 1, **Introduction**, takes you through the history of NW.js and Electron, and the massive progress the Web has made in recent years. After comparing multiple approaches to building a desktop application, you'll be guided through making your first Electron app.

Chapter 2, **The different processes**, explains how an Electron app is effectively split in two between your main process and your renderer process. Each process has its own purpose and restrictions, but we'll also show you how to communicate between them.

Chapter 3, **Using Node modules**, explores Node.js' module system as well npm, Node.js' package manger, which is by far the most popular packager manager there is. From requiring other modules, to using built-in Node modules or installing some from npm, we've got you covered.

Chapter 4, **Application lifecycle**, takes you on a journey through what happens from when your app launches until the final window is closed. You'll discover a few important events along the way.

Chapter 5, **Building a real desktop app**, takes you through building a Markdown editor with Electron, including using some of the desktop integrations previously covered.

Chapter 6, **Platform detection and custom frames**, shows you how to figure out which operating system the app is currently running on, its version, its distribution, and more. You'll also learn how to implement a custom window frame, and why that's not always such a good idea.

Chapter 7, **Desktop integrations**, shows you how tightly Electron apps can integrate into the desktop environment. From custom menus to native notifications and automatically launching your app on startup, you'll see how much more powerful an Electron app is over a Web app.

Chapter 8, **Debugging**, takes you through using the developer tools that can be used to step through the application code, tweak the DOM, profile apps, and more. We'll also revisit inter-process communication for debugging purposes.

Chapter 9, **Using Native Node modules**, explains what native modules are and why they're useful. You'll learn how to create and use a native module to dip down to a lower level.

Chapter 10, **Electron versus the Web**, explores the cutting-edge of the Web today, issues you might run into when using Web technologies on the desktop, as well as a few tips for using a single code base for the Web and the desktop.

Chapter 11, **Distributing your app**, gives you a comprehensive rundown on what's involved in creating and distributing your app to end users. This includes how to detect the current platform, how to create installers, the lessons learned, and more.

Chapter 12, **Automatic updates**, gets into the details of automatically updating your app, comparing multiple different solutions, adding client-side hooks, and learning about various server-side implementations. We'll explore other custom options, the built-in auto-updater, and how to use the Mac App Store.

Chapter 13, **Crash Reports**, shows how to automatically gather information about crashes after delivering your app to end users, including the server implementation for aggregating the reports.

About the authors

Adam Lynch is a full-stack developer from Cork, Ireland. He thinks he's funny. He's hyper, annoyingly enthusiastic, and an absolute perfectionist. He's the Head of Teamwork Chat at Teamwork.com by day and night, yet claims to be an open source contributor. Over the years, Adam has experienced a broad range of technologies, processes, and companies. This makes him painstakingly opinionated and assertive. Trust me, don't get him started. He really loves what he does. He even thinks he can do a bit of design too (hmm, yeah right). As a merciless reporter of bugs, the maintainer of a few desktop app tooling projects, and a member of the NW.js team, you'll be lucky not to come across him on GitHub while developing an NW.js or Electron app. Really lucky. I wouldn't read anything this fraud has written. You've been warned.

Max Gfeller is a web-developer from Basel, Switzerland. He currently works for a Swiss webhosting company where he develops the company's own control panel on the frontend and backend side. He's currently occupied running his own startup with a friend, where they develop software for jurists and lawyers. Electron is his go-to technology for building everyday projects. Max is very passionate about open source and in his spare free time he likes to go mountain biking or running.

Acknowledgements

Adam Lynch

I'd like to thank everyone at Bleeding Edge Press, particularly Troy Mott and Christina Rudloff, for the opportunity to put my name on a book as well as their time and efforts spent making it happen. I really appreciate it. Thank you Vladimir Krivosheev, Stefan Judis, and Paul Betts, for entertaining my questions. Roger Wang, Cheng Zhao, and everyone has contributed to NW.js, Electron, or open-source in general, I am extremely grateful for everything you have done. I'm not sure where we would be without your efforts. This book is an attempt to give something (small) back.

I'd like to thank my friends, family, colleagues, and especially my girlfriend for your patience and support while I wrote this book. A special shout-out has to go to the University careers service person who told me that "companies don't want the skills that you have," as well as whomever introduced me to the Dunning-Kruger effect; it makes me work harder every day. Finally, thank you for reading. It means a lot.

Max Gfeller

Writing this book was a great opportunity and I want to thank everyone at Bleeding Edge Press for making that happen and also for all the patience they had with me. Thanks to my friends and co-workers at cyon, the company where I work at. They did not only show great interest in what i'm doing, but they also had a lot of understanding for all the time I needed to write this book. Also, thank you to my friends at lexferenda, the startup I'm running, for their patience and interest and sometimes my lack of time to contribute more to core work.

A big thanks to all the maintainers and contributors of Atom and Electron. What you've built is truly awesome and has already saved me hundreds of hours of work. I also want to spend a special "thank you" to my wonderful girlfriend and my friends who were all very understanding that I didn't have that much time for them while writing this book and they also showed great interest. And last (but surely not least) thank you to everyone who reads this book. Please let me know if you've built something great afterwards!

Technical reviewers

We would like to the thank the following technical reviewers for their early feedback and careful critiques.

Ben Gotow is a contributor to Electron and works on Nylas N1, a mail client built on Electron. Before joining Nylas, he spent five years building native iOS and Mac applications.

Kevin Martin is an an entrepreneur who decided to experiment with Node.js around v0.4.0 and fell in love. He has been developing server-side JS ever since and Electron for the past year.

Mario Zaizar is a a Ruby developer, working with large Rails applications since 2009. He attended a talk about Atom last year and and became interested (including Electron) since then. He has contributed a few commits to Atom's documentation.

Raka Mahesa is currently a programmer for Chocoarts (**http://chocoarts.com/**), a game studio that creates games for mobile and PC. He is usually the one responsible for building new technology for the games that the studio is working on, whether it's networking, creating a map editor, or even integrating VR. He also creates his own personal apps and games in his spare time.

Code examples

All code snippets and example apps in the book can be found on GitHub at https://github.com/adam-lynch/developing-an-electron-edge.

Introduction 1

Between 2012 and the end of this year, the number of Internet users worldwide is expected to have doubled to some five billion people, and most of those will be on mobile devices in emerging markets. Interesting challenges are ahead, but it's amazing how far we've come.

The *Salmon of Knowledge*, a story from Irish mythology, really puts our progress in perspective. It centers around a salmon that has gained all of the world's knowledge. As the myth goes, the first person to taste its flesh will gain this knowledge. After seven long years of fishing, a (patient) poet named Finn Eces manages to finally catch it. Finn gives the fish to his servant, with a warning not to eat it. While cooking it, the servant noticed a bubble forming on the skin of the salmon and broke it, burning his thumb in the progress. He quickly stuck his thumb in his mouth, and to the disappointment of Finn, gained the wisdom of the salmon. Possessing all of the world's knowledge, the servant went on to become the leader of the *Fianna*, the famed band of warriors.

These days, we each have our own "Salmon of Knowledge" in our pockets. And, we use it to look at photos of cats.

The Web is a massive part of everyday life. We have an expansive reservoir of information at our fingertips, so we are more connected than ever, and we take it for granted. We can answer pretty much any question we like, which is amazing when you think about what your parents or your grandparents had.

This is partly thanks to the amazing progress Web browsers and the Web platform in general have made in such a short time. It's now possible to realize quite complex projects, with Web technologies, which were simply unimaginable just a few short years ago. It's really difficult these days to keep up; between swift introductions of increasingly powerful APIs, and the appearance of a new JavaScript framework every other day. Unreal Engine 3 was even ported to JavaScript and WebGL, making it possible to play great games directly in the browser. Blink, and you'll miss something. In Chapter 10, *Electron versus the Web*, we'll take a look at the bleeding edge of the Web today.

Web technologies, including JavaScript, are being applied in more and more interesting ways every day. Take a look at **Johnny-Five** for example; a JavaScript robotics and IoT (Internet of Things) programming framework. Not too long ago, JavaScript was despised by many. Its poor reputation stemmed from what seemed its typical use; something malicious or something really really annoying. An embarrassing amount of users intentionally disabled JavaScript in their Web browsers completely. "JavaScript" was a dirty word.

Things are very different now. JavaScript is ubiquitous and frankly, over-used. Web pages have become Web *applications*, and many Web applications will not function without JavaScript.

> *Atwood's Law*: Any application that can be written in JavaScript, will eventually be written in JavaScript.

ECMAScript 5 was published in December 2009 and is implemented by all major Web browsers and platforms. ECMAScript being standard that defines JavaScript. The sixth edition of ECMAScript, also known as ES2015, was officially published in June 2015. Inspired by CoffeeScript, Haskell, and more, a lot of nice features have been added to the language.

Most major browsers today support this standard, to varying degrees, with some features yet to be implemented. Google Chrome gladly belongs to the group of browsers that are the quickest with implementing the standard. In this book we'll be working with the current implementation of Chromium, so you'll see some proper ES2015 code.

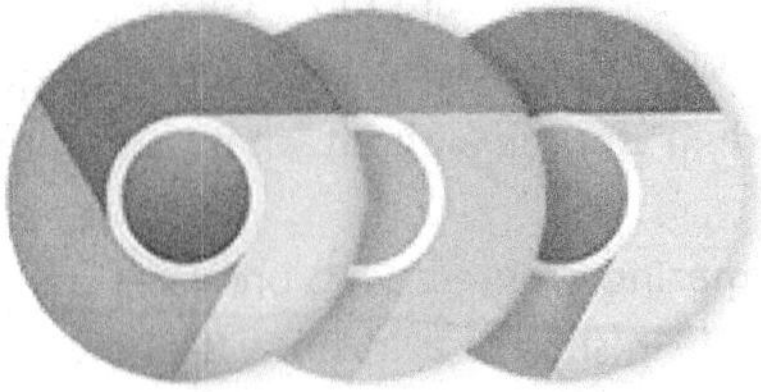

Google was already a household name by 2008 when they released Chromium, an open source Web browser project. It was built with tabs, speed, and minimalism in mind. The name comes from the element, the metal, from which chrome plating (or chrome) is made. Along with Chromium, came (Google) Chrome. It rapidly gained traction and has remained massively popular ever since.

There isn't much difference between Google Chrome and Chromium. They differ when it comes to their licenses and Chrome has some additional closed source components, like its Flash player.

Originally, both browsers shared the same rendering engine as Apple's Safari to display Web pages: WebKit. The Chromium team became the biggest contributor to WebKit, but eventually decided to leave the project in favor of their own fork named "Blink." This allowed them greater freedom in implementing features and simplifying the codebase, i.e. removing components that weren't used by Chromium. The Opera browser has since adopted Blink as well.

The speed at which these projects move is staggering. Chromium has nightly releases. Google Chrome updates less frequently but still massively much more often than other browsers before it. Updates are applied automatically when released, which is key. As one of the first "evergreen browsers," you probably don't know which version of Google Chrome you use every day. It's common these days for developers to support the "last two versions of Chrome." Most other browsers have followed suit. It reduces friction and facilitates rapid, continuous improvement. We'll take a close look at how to build automatic updates into your app in Chapter 12, *Automatic updates*.

There's also Google Chrome Canary, a separate browser to Chrome that you can install, with the only real difference that it subscribes to a separate (beta) update channel. Updates are pushed out to Chrome Canary earlier and more often than Google Chrome. Updates are more frequent, but less stable. It's really useful if you want to stay ahead of the curve, to test new APIs or ensure your app will be compatible with upcoming versions of Google Chrome.

A key reason for Google Chrome's success is owed to its highly performant JavaScript engine: v8. It converts JavaScript to machine code, highly optimizing it (and even dynamically re-optimizing it at runtime). It was also open sourced along with Chromium, and has since been used in many projects including Couchbase, MongoDB and Node.js.

At the time of writing this, Google Chrome has 56% of the **global browser market share**.

Node.js is a cross-platform runtime environment for creating server-side applications in JavaScript, using v8. Node is written in C++ but a lot of its core modules are written in JavaScript. It is event-driven and encourages asynchronous I/O. It was designed to optimize throughput and scalability in Web applications with many asynchronous input/output operations, and or real-time communication. Node has seen incredible adoption. Notably, PayPal has seen a massive productivity boost moving to it from Java, to LinkedIn, Netflix, and Uber, just to name a few.

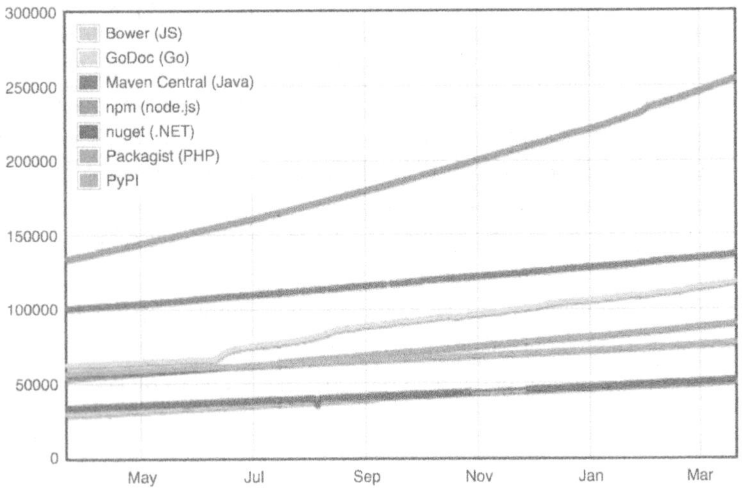

Node's package system, npm, is the largest ecosystem of open source libraries in the world. It has everything you need from automatically grabbing new dependency updates that won't break your code, a module repository you can browse on the Web, the ability to lock down dependency versions for production, and a lot more. Let's leave that for Chapter 3, *Using Node modules*.

Node and npm encourage a small module philosophy, allowing for rapid prototyping, and work really well in distributed architectures. This is partly why Node is so popular for creating microservices, a recently popularized architecture style in which complex applications are composed of small, independent pieces, communicating with each other.

JavaScript is no longer just a scripting language for the Web. It is so much more. If you wish, you can now work on a serious application all day, from top to bottom, in the one language. That's great. You can have modules that are re-used across the client-server boundary, which is even better. Universal JavaScript apps have seen a lot of success over the last couple of years. Recently, the React library has seen massive adoption, which has support for server-side rendering, which makes it way easier to progressively enhance your Web application. So, when your page loads, everything is there, functions perfectly, and then is enhanced further by client-side JavaScript. Stuff like this empowers you to make the best app you can possibly make while still being responsible. It also brings some nice performance benefits to the table too.

So you want to create a desktop app

Typically, creating a desktop application is not an appealing prospect for a Web developer. As much as we love the Web, locally installed desktop applications are certainly not dead. They're traditionally more powerful than Web apps, integrating deeply into the user's machine and desktop environment. They can tap into the filesystem, native APIs, launch on startup, and more.

Sure, there are emerging Web APIs that afford us some of the same capabilites, but we can't use them all yet. Not all browsers have added support for them yet, and a lot of people still use legacy browsers every day.

If you want an app that doesn't depend on a network connection, a desktop app is still currently the way to go. If you were to temporarily lose connectivity, you don't need the Internet to browse and play MP3s from the filesystem, for example, or you might want to create an internal app for your company that isn't exposed to the Internet at all.

Besides all of that, some users just prefer desktop applications.

Not long ago, it took an awful lot of effort to create desktop apps. More so than the cross-browser compatibility struggle. Your users will be spread over multiple operating systems, requiring a separate implementation for each target OS, e.g. Windows and Mac. Not only is this time-consuming, but you'll also need to master multiple alien languages and frameworks. And you don't want to forget your Linux users, so you'll need to maintain a Linux port of your application, too.

Some native libraries like Qt do exist, which make it possible to create multi-platform desktop applications. However, in the beginning of Qt, these had to be written in C/C++, which wasn't ideal for Web developers. We needed something a bit more approachable.

Why can't we create complex desktop apps using Web technologies? Well actually, that idea isn't new. It has been attempted multiple times already. The most well-known being Adobe Air, based on WebKit. It used ActionScript 3.0 internally (another implementation of ECMAScript) and the Flash Player rendering engine. There are some notable applications that were built with it like TweetDeck or the eBay desktop application. Linux support was dropped in 2011.

Adobe went on to create a text editor for the Web developers; Adobe Brackets. Chromium was used again, well Chrome Embedded Framework (CEF) more accurately. The user interface was written in HTML, CSS, and JavaScript. Brackets Shell, the underlying CEF application shell, was open sourced along with Brackets itself, allowing users to create their own desktop apps from Web apps. The Brackets Shell project saw some adoption, although the team behind it was very clear that it was "only maintained for use by the Brackets project," which drove a lot of developers away.

Along came node-webkit, which was a game changer. Created in 2011 by Roger Wang of Intel, it pulled Node.js and Chromium together into a very attractive package. Your app would be rendered using Blink, JavaScript ran using v8, and if you want to interact with the filesystem, hardware, and or operating system, you use Node APIs. Not only could you design and script a desktop app like you would a Web app, you also could harness the full power of Node. It practically exploded in popularity. It's no wonder that notable applications like WhatsApp, Facebook's Messenger, and Wunderlist were all built on top of NW.js. And yet, if you wanted to do something truly natively, you still could. You can drop down to C++ via Node.js, which we'll cover in more detail in Chapter 9, *Using native Node modules*.

There are, however, some downsides. There are always downsides. As you're effectively shipping Chrome plus your own code to end users, your executables are heavy. Even though it's popular, NW.js remains a little unstable. Some APIs that were released a long time ago have obvious little bugs. A recent update contained a fix for a three and a half year old bug. Unfortunately, the popularity of the project didn't translate into contributions, as most of the project is written in C++. Nevertheless, the NW.js team deserves a lot of respect for what they have achieved, and they continue to make great strides.

When GitHub decided it wanted to release their own text editor, Atom, they wanted to be able to write it from the beginning solely using Web technologies. It's what their developers were skilled at. Cheng Zhao at GitHub, who was a massive contributor to the node-webkit project at the time, decided to create a fork of node-webkit under the name "atom-shell". In making Atom, GitHub improved atom-shell greatly. If a NW.js user looks at Chapter 7, *Desktop Integrations*, they will immediately notice that a few APIs between NW.js and Electron are very similar, with key improvements, alongside the additional APIs added since the fork.

Now rebranded as Electron and pushed by GitHub, it's going from strength to strength. The Electron project on GitHub has 28,000 stars to date and over one million active users. As well as Atom, Microsoft's Visual Studio Code editor, Slack's desktop apps, and Kitematic by Docker, there are many many slick Electron apps out there.

One interesting one is **Tofino**, an internal Mozilla project with the aim of radically improving Web browsers, specifically exploring new ways of interacting with browsers. Yes you read that right; a team within Mozilla, the company behind Firefox, decided to use Electron (basically Chromium) for a project.

Electron makes the difficult parts of native desktop applications easy:

- Native menus & notifications - Chapter 7, *Desktop Integrations*
- Debugging & Profiling - Chapter 8, *Debugging*
- Crash reporting - Chapter 13, *Crash Reporting*
- Built-in auto-updater - Chapter 12, *Automatic Updates*
- Good tooling, including the ability to easily create Windows installers - Chapter 11, *Distributing Your App*

In this book, we're going to cover absolutely everything you need to know in order to make a great desktop app with Electron. Now let's get on with it.

Support and community

The first thing that separates Electron from the rest is its documentation. It's fantastic. Take a look at electron.atom.io. It's clear, beautiful, versioned, and accessible from pretty much anywhere. An edit link at the bottom of each page invites you to contribute and the community sure has accepted that invitation. The documentation is now available in ten languages and is even mirrored in China.

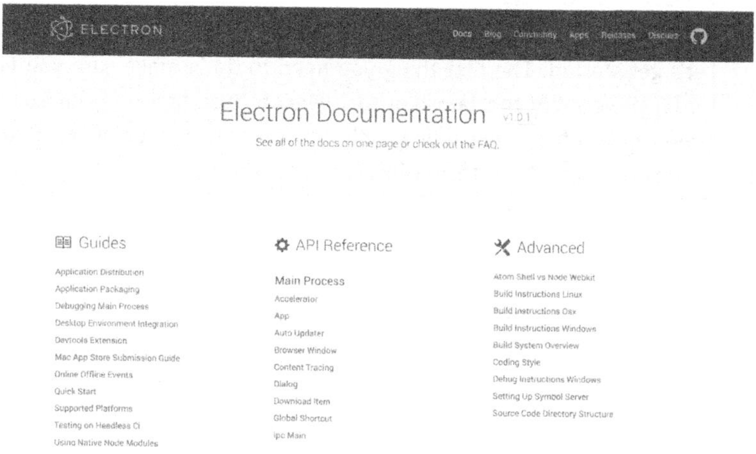

We'll cover how to build and distribute a rich desktop application from start to finish in this book, but the documentation is a great reference nevertheless. There are great breakdowns of built-in modules and the accompanying examples really go the extra mile. Don't worry if you run into a problem and the documentation isn't enough though, there's help on hand. The Electron community is alive and buzzing. Check out the **Atom forum's `electron` category**, the **Atom Slack channel** (and it's **Brazilian Portuguese equivalent**), or the `#atom-shell` channel on Freenode if IRC is more your thing.

The project maintainers are on their toes too. If you were to report a bug (by creating an issue in the **Electron project on GitHub**), expect quick replies and prompt resolution. Keep an eye on the **Atom blog** for Electron updates too.

Electron is a funny project in that it's for developers but is written in languages that are alien to most of its users. Despite this, it keeps on delivering. The team behind it are good at bridging the gap. Work on upcoming features and releases is transparent (checklists are often found in GitHub issues). There are good guides to building Electron that come in handy if, for example, you see that they're in need of someone to test something on Windows for the next release.

Inspiration isn't something you'll need to spend long looking for either. There is Sindre Sorhus' **Awesome Electron**, which is a list of great Electron apps curated by the community, to template projects and Yeoman / Slush generators to get you up and going on an Electron project quickly.

Hello, World!

Let's get started! The first thing you need to do is make sure you have Node, preferrably the latest or LTS version, installed on your system. There is an official installer which can be downloaded from **https://nodejs.org**, and this is the easiest way to install Node.

Make sure you have Node correctly installed by running `node -v`, which should show you the Node version you have running on your system. Also make sure you have npm installed, which comes bundled with Node, by running `npm -v`.

Now, make a new folder in your working directory and run `npm init`. Choose a simple name like "electron-first-steps," for the main script "main.js," and for the rest you can use default values. You should now have a `package.json` file that looks like this:

```
{
  "name": "electron-first-steps",
  "version": "1.0.0",
  "description": "",
  "main": "main.js",
  "scripts": {
    "test": "echo \"Error: no test specified\" && exit 1"
  },
  "author": "Max Gfeller",
  "license": "ISC"
}
```

Now you need to install Electron in order to run the application. Do so by running `npm install electron-prebuilt --save-dev`. The `--save-dev` flag adds this package to your list of dev-dependencies in your `package.json` file.

And let's create a `start` script, too. In the `package.json` file we can define certain scripts that can easily be run with the `npm run` command. Add this string to the "scripts" field in your `package.json` file:

```
"start": "electron ."
```

Now create a new file called `index.html` and insert the following text in it:

```
<!doctype html>
<html>
<head>
```

```
    <meta charset="utf-8">
    <title>My first Electron app</title>
  </head>
  <body>
    <h1>Hello World!</h1>
  </body>
  </html>
```

This is the main file that our application is going to display. You now need to write the code to display this HTML file when the application starts up. Modify the `main.js` as follows:

```
const electron = require('electron');
const app = electron.app;
const BrowserWindow = electron.BrowserWindow;

var mainWindow = null;

app.on('ready', () => {
  mainWindow = new BrowserWindow({ width: 800, height: 600 })

  mainWindow.loadURL('file://' + __dirname + '/index.html');
})
```

You may have noticed that we used some ES2015 code in the example above. `const` is used to assign a read-only variable. The variable cannot be reassigned.

Also there is an arrow function as callback for the `app.on()` call. This is not only a nicer way to define inline functions, but it also shares the lexical `this` with its outer scope.

Our application is now ready like this and you can try to run it by executing `npm start`. You should now see a small window that displays "Hello World."

And that is how easy Electron is to use! In the next chapters we'll go into more detail on how Electron works, and we'll build a complex app together!

The Different Processes 2

As you've seen in the *Introduction*, building a simple Electron application is actually easy! You've already used the two different types of processes that Electron knows: the main process and the renderer process. In this chapter you will learn about both processes as you build a reference to one of the earliest and most basic computer games. So let's get started!

The Main Process

You've already seen the first type of process, the `main` process in action. This is the one defined in the `package.json` file as your main process (here is an example):

```
{
  [...]
  "main": "app.js",
  [...]
}
```

The main process has direct access to all of the modules that provide certain desktop-specific logic, such as Auto Updating, Crash Reporting or opening system dialogs. All of these functionalities are described in detail in later chapters.

In the main process you'll have all of the logic for the lifecycle of your application, such as what happens when your application is started up, when it crashes (if that happens), when it's properly quitting, or when a user drags a specific file into it.

The Renderer Process(es)

The renderer process displays webpages and serves as the graphical component of an Electron application. The main process can start one or multiple renderer processes. Most of the time you'll have just one renderer process that serves as the main graphical user interface for your application.

A new browser window can be opened from the main process:

```
const BrowserWindow = require('browser-window');

var win = new BrowserWindow({ width: 800, height: 600 });
win.loadURL('file://' + __dirname + '/index.html');
```

This will open a new browser window and open the local file URL "file:///path/to/your/dir/index.html". `BrowserWindow` can take many different arguments for its constructor, and we'll explain the most important ones here.

With `width` and `height` you can specify the window's dimensions and with `x` and `y` you can set the window's offset to the left/top end of the screen. If you want to display the window just in the middle of the screen, you can use `center: true`.

There are many more options documented in the **official API docs for `browser-window`**, but one important option is `node-integration`.

Usually when you open a browser window and run some JavaScript code in it, you can use all of the APIs implemented in your browser. With the `node-integration` mode enabled (default is `true`), you'll also be able to run Node code in the browser window. Just imagine writing a Web server using Node's `http` module in a *browser* window (this allows you to start a webserver inside your webpage).

It also allows you to `require()` modules as you do in the main process. There are, however, a few drawbacks.

Certain libraries don't work with `node-integration` enabled. Scripts like jQuery check for a `CommonJS` like module system to be present and then won't register themselves as a global variable. This workaround, though, does the trick for jQuery (in the renderer process' JavaScript code):

```
window.$ = require('jquery');
```

Besides a few library incompatibilities, it can be a serious security issue. If an attacker is able to inject a `<script>` tag inside your browser window, because of unsanitized database input or a breach of an API you're using, they have access to the `fs` module, and therefore direct access to your filesystem.

The obvious solution here is to not use `node-integration` if you don't really need it. And, if you need only certain parts of it, then this is possible with the `preload` script: this takes a string of an absolute path to a script file that is being executed before other scripts run in the window. And it will always have access to Node APIs no matter if the `node-integration` is set to `true` or not. You can, for example, assign modules you know you'll be using to browser variables so that you can use them later, despite not having access to Node's APIs.

For this example we're using Electron's very own `ipc` module, which enables inter-process communication, such as sending messages and running synchronous and asynchronous tasks between different processes in your application. It consists of two parts: the `ipcMain` module for the main process and the `ipcRenderer` to use in a renderer process.

Because the `ipcRenderer` module is the only module we use in our renderer script, we don't really need `nodeIntegration` set to `true`.

Let's create `preload.js`, which will be loaded before every other script in our browser window and has full access to Node, even if `nodeIntegration` is set to `false`:

```
window.ipcRenderer = require('electron').ipcRenderer;
```

This one line is all that we need. We're using Node's `require()` function to get access to Electron's `ipcRenderer` module and assign it to the globally available `window` object. This provides inter-process communication without giving the browser window full Node access.

Let's take a look at the `main.js` script:

```
const electron = require('electron');
const app = electron.app;
const BrowserWindow = electron.BrowserWindow;
const ipcMain = electron.ipcMain;

var mainWindow = null;

// listen for the "ping" event
ipcMain.on('ping', function (event, arg) {
  if (arg === 'hello') {
```

```
      // send back a greeting
      event.sender.send('pong', 'Hello, World!');
    }
  });

  app.on('ready', () => {
    mainWindow = new BrowserWindow({ width: 800, height: 600,
  webPreferences: {
      nodeIntegration: false,
      preload: __dirname + '/preload.js' // this is our
  preload script
    }});

    mainWindow.loadURL('file://' + __dirname + '/index.html');
  });
```

We're using the `ipcMain` module to listen for the `ping` event and send a greeting back as soon as it is received. The important part in this script is the `webPreferences.preload` value, where we tell it to load our preloaded script.

If everything goes well, you will have access to the `ipcRenderer` module inside the browser script:

```
window.ipcRenderer.on('pong', (event, arg) => {
  document.write('<h1>' + arg + '</h1>');
});
window.ipcRenderer.send('ping', 'hello');
```

If you run the application you should now see this:

How this differs from NW.js

There is an area where Electron and NW.js diverge. We won't go into too much detail, but NW.js is a bit more browser-oriented. The `main` property, the entry, must be an HTML file that is then rendered in the initial window. You may hide this window, but you must have one. Scripts in or linked to this main HTML file have access to both Web and Node APIs. This window and any additional windows spawned can access the same Node.js context. Unlike Electron, your application will quit when the last remaining window is closed.

In order to achieve Node integration like this in Web pages, Chromium needs to be patched. This makes it harder for NW.js to keep up with v8, Chromium, and therefore Electron. On each new release, the NW.js team needs to patch Chromium again, add their hooks, and carefully test it.

Summary

You have now learned something about the two different kinds of Electron processes and how they can interact. This is very important for later chapters, because the renderer process does not support all of the APIs that the main process does and we therefore need a good way to call functions and interact between the main process and different renderer processes. Oh and did you get the hint to Pong, one of the first (if not the very first) computer games?

Using Node Modules 3

In the last chapter we learned a lot about the Electron process. In this chapter, we look at another basic feature you can use in Electron: Node modules. Because Electron is built on top of Node, you can use Node modules in your Electron applications.

With over 200,000 packages and nearly 3 million monthly downloads, **npm**, the package manager/registry for Node, is the biggest and fastest growing package registry in the world! Many people have written packages to solve specific needs with Node and they let others use them too by publishing them.

This is interesting, because you can enhance Node and Electron's functionality significantly with such packages, and if you want to make use of a special service or API in your application, chances are high that there already exists a module that does exactly that.

In this chapter you'll learn how to use packages from npm and also Node's internal modules. And we will tell you a trick or two on how to find really good modules on the npm registry.

Node internal modules

Node is built on the promise that it ships with the most important modules itself, and other modules that don't need to be in core are published to npm. This makes the core very lean, unlike other programming languages that strive to offer functions for every possible thing a user could ever want to do.

The documentation for all built-in modules can be found in the official **Node API documentation**. Those modules include `crypto` for basic cryptographic algorithms, `fs` to make file system operations, `http` and `https` to create http/https servers and make requests, and `net` to perform low-level network operations.

The following example shows how to read a file and display its contents using Node's internal `fs` module:

```
const fs = require('fs');

fs.readFile(__dirname + '/file.txt', function (error,
contents) {
  if (error) return console.error(error);

  console.log(contents);
});
```

Packages from npm

npm is where all the magic happens. There are packages for most anything that Node core can't already do, and it is easy to use them inside your own project.

The npm registry strives to be open to all packages for the Web platform, so you'll also find ones that don't even have JavaScript code in them and only contain CSS or HTML code. However, the majority of packages on npm are written in JavaScript or a language that compiles to JavaScript, like CoffeeScript or Babel.

Most of these packages can also be used inside Electron applications. Your application's dependencies are being defined in your `package.json` file in the `dependencies`(or `devDependencies`) section:

```
{
  "name": "my-cool-application",
  "version": "1.0.0",
  "dependencies": {
    "lodash": "^3.1.2"
  },
  "devDependencies": {
    "uglify-js": "^2.4.3"
  }
}
```

In the `dependencies` field you find all of the modules that are required to run your application, while in the `devDependencies` field only the modules required while developing the application are found.

Installing a module is easy, and the best way to do this is with the `npm install` command:

```
npm install lodash --save
```

The `install` command directly downloads the latest version into your `node_modules/` folder. The `--save` flag means that this dependency should also be directly written into your `package.json` file. You can define a specific version to download by using the following notation:

`npm install lodash@1.*` or even `npm install lodash@1.1`

To use a specific package in your code, you need to use the `require()` command.

If you take the example from above, you can require the `foo.js` module from `app.js` like this:

```
var foo = require('./foo');
```

Almost always, the `require()` function will look in the `node_modules/` folder of your application for the required module. If it doesn't find the package there it will look for a `node_modules/` folder level above, and if it won't find one there it will throw an error. In our example above, `node_modules` is not searched because the path begins with a dot, therefore making it a relative path.

Semantic Versioning

When you define your application's dependencies in your `package.json` file you can specify certain version ranges for each package. If you specify version `1.*` it will always install the latest version of this package that falls into this range.

Most packages on npm do follow the **SemVer** specification that can easily be described like this:

```
Major.Minor.Patch
```

or even easier:

```
Breaking.Feature.Fix
```

That means if something in a package changes and actually breaks something in it's API, then it's developers release a new major version of their library. If they introduce a new feature that does not break the existing API, they release a new minor version, and if they just fix things that don't really have an effect on it's API, then they release a new patch version.

Normally you would pin your dependencies by their major versions, and if you run `npm update` you will always get the newest features. The problem with this approach is that not every package developer can be this trustworthy and may from time to time break a package's API without releasing a new major version.

The solution to this is the `npm shrinkwrap` command: it saves the *exact* installed version in a `npm-shrinkwrap.json` file. If you distribute your application and one of your users or fellow developers runs `npm install`, they will get the exact same dependencies.

Finding good packages

If you're looking for a package to use for a specific need that you have, searching on the **npm Website** will lead to many results. And with over 200,000 packages published, not all of them have the same quality.

So, how can you tell the good ones from the not so good ones? Well, that is something that usually comes with experience, but there are also some points that help you see if a package is great or not so great:

- *A README file:* all good packages have a README file that explains how to use the module.
- *Single concern:* a great module usually only does one thing. It doesn't try to solve all of your problems.
- *Tests:* Automated tests that can be run using `npm test` are usually provided by good packages.
- *Doesn't have too many open issues on Github:* Too many open Github issues are usually not a sign of a good package, especially if they are open for a long time.

Many people will tell you that the author of a module is also very important, but it's hard to tell what's a great module author when you're new to Node. And often, authors of one great module only maintain one, because they use it themselves and don't publish many modules.

Summary

You have learned how to use Node's internal modules and even modules from the npm registry. If you write a real world desktop application with Electron, chances are you're depending on hundreds of different packages. All of them are defined in your `package.json` file and with `npm shrinkwrap` you've learned about a tool to pin down the exact versions of the packages you've installed. This is especially useful when you're writing an application with many dependencies and you can't really guarantee that they all follow the Semantic Versioning scheme.

We'll use modules from npm through the whole book, and in a later chapters we're even going to learn how to use Native Addons (modules written in C/C++)!

Application Lifecycle 4

In the last chapter we covered how to use Node modules, and in the next chapter we will walk through creating a real-world application, but first we need to cover a few more essential Electron topics. In this chapter we look at the basic lifecycle of an Electron application. What happens when you start an application? And what happens when it stops running? At the end of the chapter you'll know at which point during execution multiple handlers get initialized, and where you have to disconnect to databases.

Before your Code is loaded

Electron bundles a Chromium and a Node runtime to make it possible to write desktop applications using Web technologies. So what happens exactly when you start an Electron application?

Well, it turns out a lot happens before your application code is even loaded:

- The Electron packed Node runtime is started
- All required libraries are loaded
- Your `main` module is loaded and executed

The `main` module is the one that you've defined in your `package.json` file. And while an application can spawn multiple renderer processes, there can only be one main process. It controls the whole state of your application and you can react to different events that may occur.

The one module that is responsible for controlling the application's lifecycle is the app module that you only have access to from your main process. It is an EventEmitter on which you can subscribe to certain events, and you can stop or crash your application using this module.

Let's look at the different lifecycle events in a typical Electron application.

Startup

A lot needs to be done so Electron can execute your application's code. But as soon as it's done setting up all of the required runtimes and shared libraries, and as soon as your code is loaded, the `app` module emits it's first event: the `ready` event.

Actually, the first event that is being emitted is the `will-finish-launching` event, which is the same as the `ready` event on both Windows and Linux. On Mac OS X it represents the **`applicationWillFinishLaunching` notification of `NSApplication`**.

Most of the time you probably want to use the `ready` event.

Now the `ready` event's callback is a very good place to start the application's auto updater and crash reporter. Also, the `ready` event is the right place to set up `open-file` listeners so your application can open various files.

We'll get to the point in the next chapter.

Quitting

There's a few different scenarios that can stop your application from running. The first, is that all windows you have opened from the main process have been closed (`window-all-closed`). You want to quit your application when that happens. On Mac OS X, most applications only quit when you press `Cmd + q`, so you can still let your application run even when there are no more open windows:

```
app.on('window-all-closed', () => {
  if (process.platform !== 'darwin') {
    app.quit();
  }
});
```

Usually, if the user clicks the dock icon of that application, a window reappears. You can listen to the dock click with the `activate` event:

```
app.on('activate', () => {
  if (mainWindow === null) {
```

```
    createMainWindow();
  }
});
```

Before an application quits and closes all of its windows, Electron will emit a `before-quit` event. In this event you can, for example, check for unsaved changes in documents. If you do a `evt.preventDefault()` in the callback handler, the application prevents the default behavior, which is closing all windows and quitting the application.

```
app.on('before-quit', (evt) => {
  if (hasUnsavedChanges()) {
    evt.preventDefault();
  }
});
```

When all windows have been closed already, the application will emit a `will-quit` event. The same applies to this event: you can prevent the default behavior, thus quitting the app, with `evt.preventDefault()`. The last thing your application does before it stops running is emitting the `quit` event, which also provides you with an exit code:

```
app.on('quit', (evt, exitCode) => {
  console.log('application quit with exit code:', exitCode)
});
```

Crashing

Even if you're one of the best programmers in the world, errors do happen. And it might not even be your own fault, because things can go wrong all of the time, especially in a large code base, and even more so if you're depending on a lot of external services.

Exceptions in the main process actually can get your application to crash, which is not good, even if you've set up a crash reporter. Luckily for us, the `process` EventEmitter object knows the event `uncaughtException`. So can you just use this to prevent your application from crashing? Well, it's not that easy.

Take this example:

```
const electron = require('electron');
const app = electron.app;

process.on('uncaughtException', (err) => {
```

```
  console.log('application almost crashed!', err);
});

app.on('ready', () => {
  setTimeout(() => {
    nonExistentFunc();
  }, 2000);
});
```

If you run this code, you get to the point where you can react to the uncaught exception that occurs because you mistakenly tried to call a function that was not even defined.

So this is good, right? Well, it turns out that mostly it is not.

If you use the `process.on('uncaughtException')` event listener to react to exceptions, you have no idea where an error can occur. Also, if you execute more code after you try to call your non-existent function, this won't be executed:

```
const electron = require('electron');
const app = electron.app;

process.on('uncaughtException', (err) => {
  console.log('application almost crashed!', err);
});

app.on('ready', () => {
  setTimeout(() => {
    nonExistentFunc();
    console.log('more important stuff'); // won't ever get
called
  }, 2000);
});
```

The official Node documentation has a very explicit warning on using this event:

> The event *should not* be used as an equivalent to `On Error Resume Next`. Unhandled exceptions inherently mean that an application is in an undefined state. Attempting to resume application code without properly recovering from the exception can cause additional unforeseen and unpredictable issues.

Does that mean, you shouldn't use this event? No, it can be very valuable to know about unforseen errors. But after using the logic in the callback handler of `uncaughtException`, you need to exit the application. This can be done in a friendly way by informing that there was an error, or the process can crash to invoke the defined crash reporter.

Summary

You learned that several things need to be done in order to load your application, and that there are two different events at the start of each application (that are not that different after all).

Also, you learned when you need to check if a user has unsaved work, and how to prevent the application quitting before losing all of this unsaved work. There are many events that get emitted before the application quits, in order to observe the whole quitting process.

You also learned about the `uncaughtException` event of the `process` object and what you can do in it's callback handler. And you don't want to resume a normal application procedure if there is an exception!

Keep all of this in mind, because you'll soon put it to further use!

Building a Real Desktop App 5

You've seen how Electron works, including its lifecycle and how to make use of multiple integrations on different desktop platforms, allowing you to build truly native applications.

You now have the prerequisites necessary to build a real desktop application, which we will do in this chapter. All of the code from this chapter can be found on GitHub at **github.com/adam-lynch/developing-an-electron-edge/tree/master/05-BuildingARealDesktopApp**.

Initializing the project

Let's build an editor that can edit Markdown files and save them to the filesystem. Let's begin by creating a new Electron project. Run this in a new folder:

```
npm init
npm install --save electron-prebuilt
```

Now add a `start` script to `package.json`, which will start the application:

```
scripts: {
  "start": "electron ."
}
```

Also, make sure the `main` property points to `main.js` (which we'll create shortly).

The **`marked`** module on npm is pretty popular for parsing Markdown code, and can be installed by running `npm install --save marked`.

You should now have a directory with a `package.json`, along with a `node_modules` directory containing your`electron-prebuilt` and `marked` dependencies.

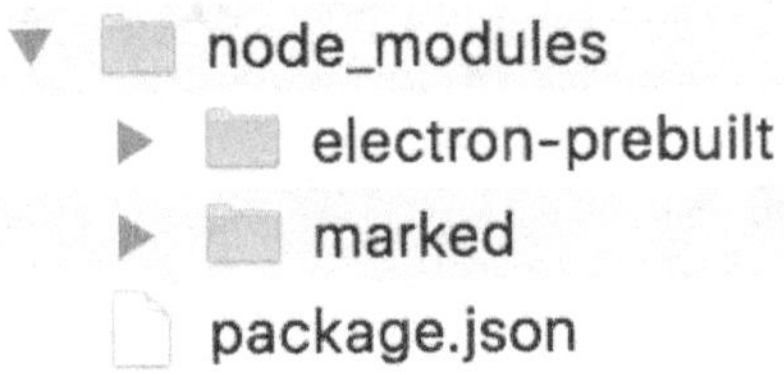

It is time to implement the editor. Let's start by creating a `main.js` at the root of the project like this:

```
const electron = require('electron');
const app = electron.app;
const BrowserWindow = electron.BrowserWindow;

var mainWindow = null;

app.on('ready', () => {
  mainWindow = new BrowserWindow({ width: 800, height:
600 });
  mainWindow.loadURL('file://' + __dirname + '/index.html');
});
```

As we covered earlier, as long as the `main` property in your `package.json` points to it, this file will be run by Electron in the "main process" when your app is launched, and will only die when your app does. The code is simple. We're opening a new window and loading an `index.html` (which we've yet to write).

The frontend

Let's create the frontend. This is a simple `index.html` file, again to go at the root of the project:

```
<!doctype html>
<html>
<head>
  <meta charset="utf-8">
  <title>Our cool editor</title>
```

```
    <link rel="stylesheet" href="style.css">
  </head>
  <body>
    <main>
      <div class="container">
        <div class="editor">
          <textarea autofocus="true" placeholder="# Write
something here..."></textarea>
        </div>
        <div class="preview"></div>
      </div>
    </main>
    <script type="text/javascript" src="index.js"></script>
  </body>
</html>
```

As you can see, there's a `textarea` for editing and also a `div` for previewing the result. Here's some minimal CSS for the editor, which goes in a new `style.css` stylesheet (at the root as well):

```
body {
  margin: 0;
  padding: 0;
  font-family: sans-serif;
}

.container {
  width: 100%;
  height: 100vh;
  display: block;
}

.editor,
.preview {
  box-sizing: border-box;
  padding: 10px;
}

.editor {
  width: 50%;
  height: 100%;
  float: left;
}

.editor textarea {
  resize: none;
  border: none;
  outline: none;
```

```
  width: 100%;
  height: 100%;
}

.preview {
  width: 50%;
  height: 100%;
  float: left;
  padding-left: 2px;
  margin-left: -2px;
  background-color: #ddd;
}
```

This gives us the editor on the left and the live preview on the right side. If you're following along, your project directory should now look something like this:

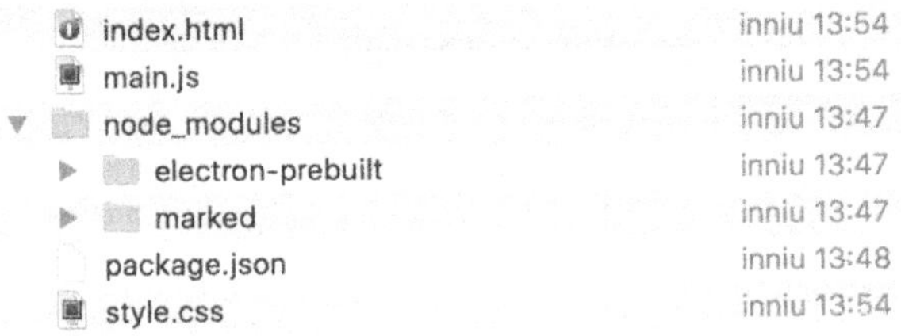

Adding logic

Now all that's missing is the client-side logic. All we need is an `index.js` as the window loads `index.html`, and as you might have spotted in its source code, `index.html` loads `index.js` with a `script` tag.

In `index.js`, let's listen to changes in the `textarea`, re-generate the Markdown, and display it.

```
const marked = require('marked');

const editor = document.querySelector('.editor textarea');
const preview = document.querySelector('.preview');

marked.setOptions({
  gfm: true,
  tables: true,
  breaks: false,
  pedantic: false,
```

```
  sanitize: true,
  smartLists: true,
  smartypants: false
});

editor.onkeyup = generatePreview;

function generatePreview () {
  var content = editor.value;
  var html = marked(content);
  preview.innerHTML = html;
}
```

(For all available options of `marked`, check out its **documentation on the npm site**).

If you run the whole thing, you'll discover that we already have a fully working Markdown editor.

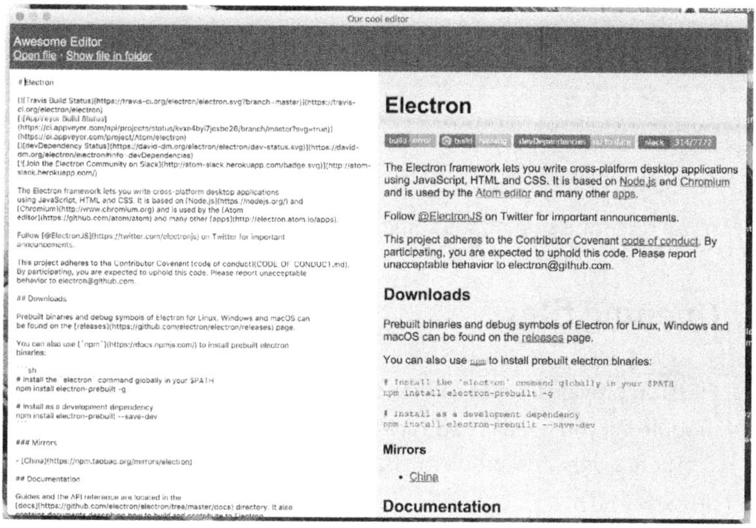

This is great, but let's enhance the application so it can open Markdown files and edit them!

There's a few things we must do in order to make this possible. First of all, let's hide the editor and previewer if there isn't any file open:

```
<div class="container hidden">
  <div class="editor">
    <textarea autofocus="true" placeholder="# Write
something here..."></textarea>
```

```
    </div>
    <div class="preview"></div>
  </div>
```

This is the same HTML as in `index.html` from earlier, but notice the `hidden` class we've added to the container.

Now add this small snippet to the `style.css` file:

```
.hidden {
  display: none;
}
```

Also, add a link to open a file:

```
<div class="header">
  <div class="title">Awesome Editor</div>
  <a href="#" class="open-file">Open file</a>
</div>
```

And the CSS for it:

```
.header a {
  color: #ddd;
}
```

All that's missing now is some logic.

Opening files

Electron provides a nice API for opening files, and more, via the `dialog` module. All you need is `require('electron').dialog` to access it.

There's only one problem. This module is only available to the main process (`main.js`), but not our renderer process (`index.html` and `index.js`). Luckily, there is an easy solution to this; use the `remote` module. With the `remote` module, you can invoke methods of the main process object without explicitly sending inter process messages, thus requiring modules that are only available to the main process.

You can use it like this in the `index.js` file:

```
const remote = require('remote');
const dialog = remote.require('dialog');
```

Instead of the local `require()` function, just use the one from the main process.

Now implement what happens when the user clicks the "Open File" link:

```
const openFileLink = document.querySelector('a.open-file');

openFileLink.onclick = (evt) => {
  dialog.showOpenDialog({
    title: 'Select a file to edit',
    filters: [
      { name: 'Markdown Documents', extensions: ['md',
'markdown'] }
    ]
  }, (filenames) => {
    if (!filenames) return;
    if (filenames.length > 0) {
      openFile(filenames[0]);
    }
  })
};
```

All of the `dialog.showOpenDialog` function's arguments are optional. `defaultPath` (which we have left out of the example) allows you to specify the directory the dialog should open at, and the `filters` option allows you to specify an array of file types the user can select to change which files are visible by that specific type. These are Markdown files in our case. You need to give a `name` string and an `extensions` array for each. The strings in `extensions` must either be * for all, or else the file extension (without the dot or wildcard). The `properties` array can have any or all of the following: `openFile`, `openDirectory`, `multiSelections` and`createDirectory`. These are the selection features or criteria the dialog allows.

Note: On Windows and Linux, you can't have a single dialog that allows both `openFile` and `openDirectory`.

Please note that the `filenames` argument to the callback function is only set if the user has actually selected a file. We'll just ignore it if no files are set for now.

Let's implement the `openFile()` function (which is called if a file *is* selected):

```
// add this line to the top of your file
const fs = require('fs');
```

```
// ...

function openFile (filename) {
  var contents = fs.readFileSync(filename);

  currentFile = filename;

  editor.value = contents;
  container.classList.remove('hidden');

  generatePreview();
}
```

We're using Node's `fs` module to read the file and put its contents into the editor element. Then remove the **hidden** class from the whole editor component and generate the preview.

The result looks like this:

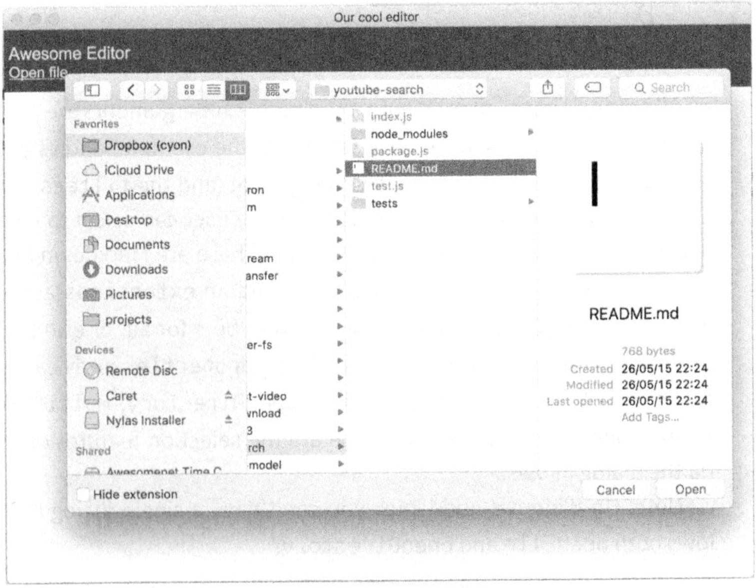

or

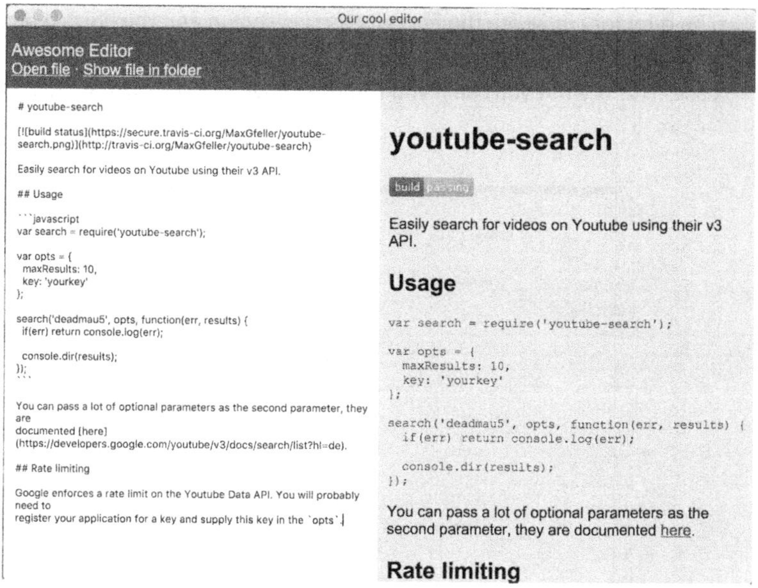

Now we have a small challenge for you: can you implement a "Save" button?

Tip: just look at the **documentation** of Node's `fs` module.

Tapping into the desktop a bit more

Now a user can open a file and edit it (and if you did your challenge, even save it again!). Let's look at some more tricks with Electron to enhance the user's experience.

Let's add a new link, which will show the current Markdown file in its folder using the system file manager.

Electron comes with a handy "Shell" module for performing operating system level actions on file paths and URLs. We'll take a look at the API in its entirety later on, but for now let's focus on one.

```
var shell = require('shell');
shell.showItemInFolder('/Users/adam/Desktop/abc/
example.txt');
```

Probably the method with the least number of use-cases, `shell.showItemInFolder`, takes a file path and reveals the file to the user with the default file browser. For example, the file's location would be opened in Windows Explorer if the method was called on Windows. The directory in which the file is located is shown and the file is typically selected, but depending on the platform or program, this may not be the case. This is what you see if you run the above snippet on Mac OS X Mavericks.

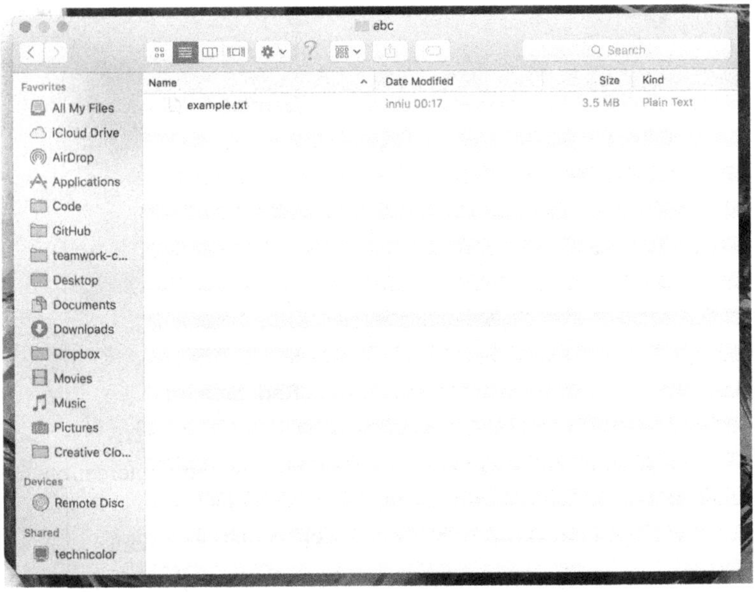

The file path can be relative or absolute, but I'd advise only passing absolute paths because we've found that relative paths may not be resolved correctly. When this happens or when you pass a file path that doesn't exist, but typically nothing happens.

So, back to our app. Let's add a link in `index.html`:

```
<div class="header">
  <div class="title">Awesome Editor</div>
  <a href="#" class="open-file">Open file</a>
  &middot;
  <a href="#" class="show-file-in-folder">Show file in
folder</a>
</div>
```

Next in `index.js`, we need to add a call to the `shell` module's `showItemInFolder()` function with the current file when the link is clicked:

```
const shell = require('electron').shell;
const showFileInFolderLink = document.querySelector('a.show-
file-in-folder');
showFileInFolderLink.onclick = (evt) => {
  shell.showItemInFolder(currentFile);
};
```

That's it!

Dropping a file on the dock icon (Mac OS X)

It's time for some more desktop integrations. What happens when a user tries to open a file with your app, such as dragging and dropping a file onto the app icon? As we've covered already, the `app` module provides events like `ready`. There's another, `open-file`, which is fired when the user has tried to open a file with your application. Here's what we need in `main.js`:

```
// add to the top of file
const app = require('electron').app;

// ...

global.fileToOpen = null;

app.on('open-file', (event, filePath) => {
  event.preventDefault();
  fileToOpen = filePath;

  if(mainWindow){
    mainWindow.send('open-file', filePath);
  }
});
```

Note: notice here that we don't listen to `ready` and then, in the callback, listen to `open-file`; it's best to listen for this event even before `ready` because it can be fired really early.

There are two cases we need to cover here: When your app isn't running (when the event is being emitted before the app is started), and when it's already running. Remember, when the app starts and the `ready` event is fired, we open the main window and store it in `mainWindow`. If `mainWindow` isn't initialized yet in the callback, it means the event was fired before the window was opened. Therefore, our app wasn't running.

So when the open-file event is emitted and mainWindow exists, we'll trigger a function in the renderer process using Electron's ipc module. The renderer process (index.js) will listen for this over ipc, but we'll take a look at that in a second.

If the app wasn't running (such as mainWindow doesn't exist), however, we'll just assign the full path to a global variable. Then when the renderer process is eventually started up (as the app is launched and the ready event is fired), it will check for this main process global variable, which is easy to access from the renderer side.

Let's take a look at what we need to add to the index.js file to handle all of that:

```
const ipcRenderer = require('electron').ipcRenderer;

var currentFile = remote.getGlobal('fileToOpen') || null;

if(currentFile){
  openFile(currentFile);
}

ipcRenderer.on('open-file', (event, filePath) => {
  openFile(filePath);
});
```

First, we're grabbing the global variable fileToOpen from the main process side if it exists. If one is set, we'll open the file for this one. Also we're registering a handler for the open-file event that can be emitted by the main process.

That's it! You can now drag files onto your dock icon, whether your application is running or not, and it should automatically be opened by the application.

Recent documents

Handling this open-file event is also necessary for the next feature we're going to build: the recent documents dock view. If you were to right-click an app in your dock or taskbar, you might see a list of items recently opened with that application.

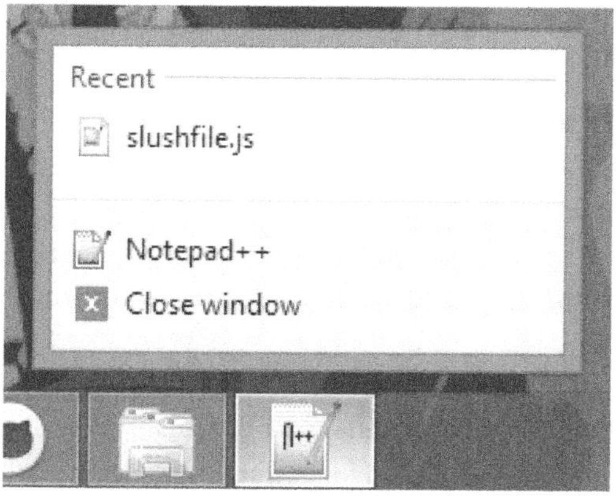

Let's enhance the application with a list of recent documents opened by the application via JumpList or the dock menu, respectively. This feature is only available to the Windows and Mac OS X platforms.

This is achieved again using Electron's `app` module, so you'll need the `remote` module once again. To add a document, call `app.addRecentDocument` with an absolute file path, so calling `app.clearRecentDocuments` will empty the list.

Add the following line to the `openFile()` function:

```
remote.app.addRecentDocument(filename);
```

That's really all that is needed. Now both Windows and Mac OS X provide you with this list of recent documents you've edited for quick access.

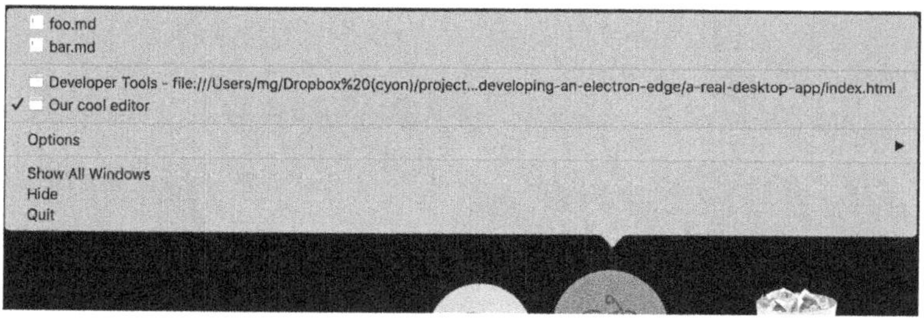

On a Mac, clicking one of the items in the list will fire the `open-file` event we went over earlier. On Windows, a new instance of your app will be opened with the file as a command-line argument.

Note: Windows only allows you to add files to the list if your app is the registered handler for that file type.

Represented file (Mac OS X)

Another very cool feature is the "represented filename." It let's you display the currently opened file in the editor in the taskbar of the application, and even shows the parent folders. This feature is unfortunately available on Mac OS X.

This needs to be called directly on the `BrowserWindow` instance, which means it needs to happen from the main process. You've already set up the interprocess communication infrastructure with `ipc`, so let's listen to a event in the main process (`main.js`):

```
ipcMain.on('set-represented-filename', (event, filename) => {
  mainWindow.setRepresentedFilename(filename);
});
```

Now you just need to call this from the renderer process (`index.js`) as soon as you open a file:

```
document.title = filename;
ipcRenderer.send('set-represented-filename', filename);
```

As you may have noticed, we also need to manually set the filename as the title of the window. The result looks like this:

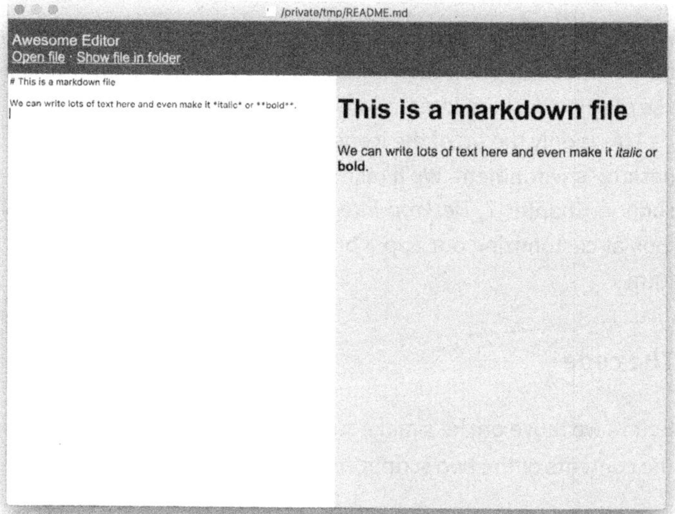

If you do a right-click on the filename, it will show you the parent folders of the opened file:

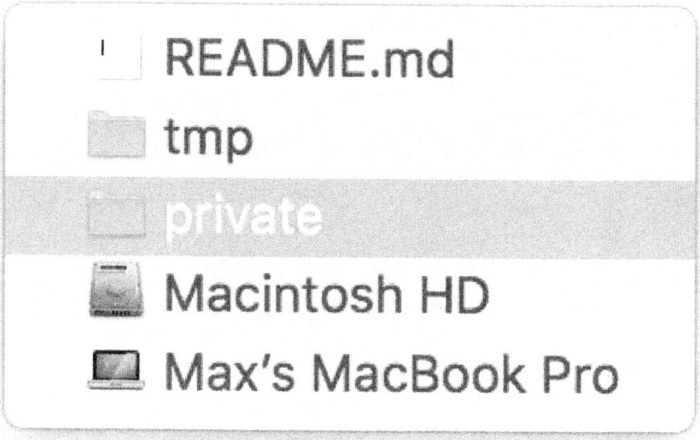

And when you click on one of the parent folders, it even opens it in the Finder.

Summary

Well done! You've written a small editor for the very popular Markdown format that can open files (and maybe even save them), which makes use of some desktop integrations.

This is only the tip of the iceberg when it comes to integrating into the desktop environment. We'll take a deep dive into the rest of your options soon in Chapter 7, *Desktop Integrations*. In the meantime, we'll take a look at customizing our app a bit further depending on the current platform.

The code

Before we move on, let's make sure we're on the same page. At this point the contents of the two scripts are as follows, `main.js`:

```
const electron = require('electron');
const app = electron.app;
const BrowserWindow = electron.BrowserWindow;

var mainWindow = null;

global.fileToOpen = null;

app.on('open-file', (event, path) => {
  event.preventDefault();
  fileToOpen = path;

  if(mainWindow){
    mainWindow.send('open-file', path);
  }
});

app.on('ready', () => {
  mainWindow = new BrowserWindow({ width: 800, height:
600 });
  mainWindow.loadURL('file://' + __dirname + '/index.html');

  // Uncomment next line to show DevTools when the app
launches
  //mainWindow.openDevTools();
});
```

`index.js`:

```
const marked = require('marked');
const remote = require('remote');
const dialog = remote.require('dialog');
const fs = require('fs');
const shell = require('electron').shell;
const ipcRenderer = require('electron').ipcRenderer;

const container = document.querySelector('.container');
const editor = document.querySelector('.editor textarea');
const preview = document.querySelector('.preview');
const openFileLink = document.querySelector('a.open-file');
const showFileInFolderLink = document.querySelector('a.show-
file-in-folder');

var currentFile = remote.getGlobal('fileToOpen') || null;

if(currentFile) {
  openFile(currentFile);
}

ipcRenderer.on('open-file', (event, arg) => {
  openFile(arg);
});

marked.setOptions({
  gfm: true,
  tables: true,
  breaks: false,
  pedantic: false,
  sanitize: true,
  smartLists: true,
  smartypants: false
});

editor.onkeyup = generatePreview;

openFileLink.onclick = (evt) => {
  dialog.showOpenDialog({
    title: 'Select a file to edit',
    filters: [
      { name: 'Markdown Documents', extensions: ['md',
'markdown'] }
    ]
  }, (filenames) => {
    if (!filenames) return;
    if (filenames.length > 0) {
      openFile(filenames[0]);
    }
  })
```

```
};

showFileInFolderLink.onclick = (evt) => {
  shell.showItemInFolder(currentFile);
};

function generatePreview () {
  var content = editor.value;
  var html = marked(content);
  preview.innerHTML = html;
}

function openFile (filename) {
  var contents = fs.readFileSync(filename);

  currentFile = filename;

  editor.value = contents;
  container.classList.remove('hidden');

  generatePreview();

  remote.app.addRecentDocument(filename);
}
```

Platform Detection and Custom Frames 6

Now let's take a look at what options we have when it comes to the chrome of our app. This includes how you can tweak the window frame, the controls, and more. To do this, you need to know about the environment our app is presently running in. In this chapter, we'll be taking a dive into the world of platform-specific styles, custom HTML controls, the ease at which you can create a custom frame, and the downsides that come with it.

First though, we need to cover platform detection.

There are various reasons why you might want to detect which platform or operating system your app is currently running on. Your keyboard shortcuts, or user interface, may differ per platform, so you might want to store files in platform-specific directories on disk. Electron's native or desktop integration APIs aren't uniform, so we'll certainly need to tweak our code per platform. Thanks to Node's `os` module, it isn't too difficult. We're going to take a look at creating a module to detect which operating system your app is currently running on, along with its version, architecture, and distribution. We also show you how to apply platform-dependent styles.

Which operating system?

On Mac, Linux and Windows, the following script stores `darwin`, `linux` and `win32` or `win64` respectively in the `platform` variable.

```
const os = require('os');
var platform = os.platform();
```

The other possible return values of `os.platform()` are `freebsd` and `sunos`. This code can be used in either the main or renderer processes.

Which Linux distribution?

Figuring this out is a bit more problematic. The `uname -v` command returns some information like the following if run on Ubuntu: `#42~precise1-Ubuntu SMP Wed Aug 14 15:31:16 UTC 2013`. You can spawn this command via Node's **`child_process`** module or any of the countless similar modules on `npm`.

It's probably safest to check for and read distrubition-specific release information files (with the Node's **`fs`** module), which include:

Distribution	File(s)
Debian	`/etc/debian_release` and `/etc/debian_version`, but be careful since these also exist on Ubuntu
Fedora	`/etc/fedora-release`
Gentoo	`/etc/gentoo-release`
Mandrake	`/etc/mandrake-release`
Novell SUSE	`/etc/SUSE-release`
Red Hat	`/etc/redhat-release` and `/etc/redhat_version`
Slackware	`/etc/slackware-release` and `/etc/slackware-version`
Solaris / Sparc	`/etc/release`
Sun JDS	`/etc/sun-release`
UnitedLinux	`/etc/UnitedLinux-release`
Ubuntu	`/etc/lsb-release` and `/etc/os-release`
Yellow dog	`/etc/yellowdog-release`

Keep in mind that the format of each of these files can differ. Here is an example `/etc/lsb-release` file:

```
DISTRIB_ID=Ubuntu
DISTRIB_RELEASE=12.04
DISTRIB_CODENAME=precise
DISTRIB_DESCRIPTION="Ubuntu 12.04.3 LTS"
```

And here is an example `/etc/os-release` file:

```
NAME="Ubuntu"
VERSION="12.04.3 LTS, Precise Pangolin"
ID=ubuntu
ID_LIKE=debian
PRETTY_NAME="Ubuntu precise (12.04.3 LTS)"
VERSION_ID="12.04"
```

Note: LSB stands for Linux Standard Base. There is also a `lsb_release` command you can run to get information like this, which is supposedly OS agnostic, but in reality it's not quite universal.

Similar to browser sniffing in the Web development world, it's probably safest not to do this and detect individual features instead. So for example, if you need to perform a certain system action, try running multiple possible commands to find the one that the current distribution supports.

32-bit or 64-bit architecture?

The safest way to check this is to use `os.arch()` in combination with system environment variables:

```
const os = require('os');
const is64Bit = os.arch() === 'x64' ||
process.env.hasOwnProperty('PROCESSOR_ARCHITEW6432');
```

Version detection

Version detection is a bit trickier. `os.release()` returns the platform version, but it's not what you'd expect it to be. It will return the actual internal operating system version. You might expect the return value to be `10.0.0` when called on Mac OSX Yosemite, but it will in fact return `14.0.0`. To see the mappings between Darwin and Mac release versions, see the ***Darwin (operating system)*** Wikipedia entry.

Microsoft **provides**.aspx) Windows' versions, but you may need to do some testing yourself to be safe, because you can see how both Windows 8 and Windows Server 2012 are both listed as being `9.2`. We find it's safe to check against `6.2.9200`.

`os.release()` will return whatever `uname -v` returns on Linux (such as `3.8.0-29-generic` on Ubuntu 12.04.3 LTS), so it's safer to read the distribution-specific release information file(s) shown earlier.

The finished article

The final version of our `platform.js` module looks like this:

```
const os = require('os');

var platform = {
  isLinux: false,
  isMac: false,
  isWindows: false,
  isWindows8: false,
  version: os.release()
};


/**
 * Checks if the current platform version is greater than or
equal to the desired minimum version given
 *
 * @param minimumVersion {string} E.g. 10.0.0.
 * See [the Darwin operating system Wikipedia entry](http://
en.wikipedia.org/wiki/Darwin_%28operating_system
%29#Release_history) for Mac - Darwin versions.
 * Also, Windows 8 >= 6.2.9200
 *
 * @returns {boolean}
 */
var isOfMinimumVersion = (minimumVersion) => {
  var actualVersionPieces = platform.version.split('.'),
    pieces = minimumVersion.split('.'),
    numberOfPieces = pieces.length;

  for(var i = 0; i < numberOfPieces; i++){
    var piece = parseInt(pieces[i], 10),
      actualPiece = parseInt(actualVersionPieces[i], 10);

    if (typeof actualPiece === 'undefined') {
```

```
      break; // e.g. 13.1 passed and actual is 13.1.0
    }
    else if (actualPiece > piece) {
      break; // doesn't matter what the next bits are, the 
major version (or whatever) is larger
    }
    else if (actualPiece === piece) {
      continue; // to check next version piece
    }
    else {
      return false;
    }
  }

  return true; // all was ok
};


var name = os.platform();

if(name === 'darwin'){
  platform.name = 'mac';
  platform.isMac = true;
}
else if(name === 'linux'){
  platform.name = 'linux';
  platform.isLinux = true;
}
else {
  platform.name = 'windows';
  platform.isWindows = true;
  platform.isWindows8 = isOfMinimumVersion('6.2.9200');
}

platform.is64Bit = os.arch() === 'x64' || 
process.env.hasOwnProperty('PROCESSOR_ARCHITEW6432');

module.exports = platform;
```

Take note of the `isOfMinimumVersion` method and the `isWindows8` property.

So, from anywhere in your app you can `require` this module and use it for platform-specific code where necessary. For example:

```
const platform = require('./platform');

if(platform.isMac){
  // do something
```

```
}
else if(platform.isWindows8 && platform.is64bit) {
  // do something else
}
```

If you're following along, make sure to add the `platform.js` file to the root of your project.

Platform-dependent styles

You may have spotted that our `platform.js` module exports a `name` property. This is really useful for applying platform-specific styles. To achieve differing styles per platform, we'll use this `name` property to add a `platform-` class to the body element:

```
const platform = require('./platform');
// ...
document.body.classList.add('platform-' + platform.name);
```

You can add this to `index.js`, since we'll be using it soon.

Note that we used **`Element.classList`** here which **isn't supported** by a lot of browsers currently in use. The great thing about Electron is you can ignore that, since it'll be fine for 100% of our app's users.

You can change the styling of certain elements based on the current platform. Stepping away from our app for a minute, let's say you have some nice custom button styles and you'd like them to be a bit rounder on Mac OS X. All you have to do is use the `platform-` class in the CSS:

```
.button {
  /* Your custom styles */
  border-radius: 3px;
}

.platform-mac .button {
  border-radius: 5px;
}
```

Hypothetically, any elements with the `button` class look just like the custom buttons you designed (or grabbed from **CodePen**), but if the `platform-mac` class exists on an ancestor, such as the body element, the buttons' corners are rounder.

You can easily go a little further and add certain classes depending on the given platform version. You can add a `platform-windows-8` class to the body if `platform.isWindows8` is `true` and then make the buttons' **square-cornered**) if it exists.

```
.button {
  /* Your custom styles */
  border-radius: 3px;
}

.platform-mac .button {
  border-radius: 5px;
}

.platform-windows-8 .button {
  border-radius: 0;
}
```

Dark mode

Since Mac OS X Yosemite, there's a new "dark mode," which gives a few things a darker theme or look, including the dock, menubar, and more. You can tweak your app based on this thanks to `app.isDarkMode`.

```
const app = require('electron').app;
const platform = require('./platform');

document.body.classList.add('platform-' + platform.name);
if(platform.isMac && app.isDarkMode()){
  document.body.classList.add('platform-' + platform.name +
'--dark');
}
```

Custom frames

An Electron app is just like an ordinary desktop app, in that it has a frame you'd expect to see that comes from the operating system. It's possible, however, to create your own custom buttons. Let's do this with the Markdown editor from earlier. First we need to turn off the default native frame (in `main.js`);

```
app.on('ready', () => {
 mainWindow = new BrowserWindow({
   width: 800,
   height: 600,
   frame: false // we've added this line
 });
 mainWindow.loadURL('file://' + __dirname + '/index.html');
});
```

As you can see, the `BrowserWindow` API takes responsibility for this, which we changed in `main.js`. You simply have to pass `frame: false` when instantiating a window to remove the native frame. To add our own, we need some HTML like this:

```
<div class="window-bar">
  <ul class="window-actions">
    <li class="window-action-wrapper"><a href="#"
class="window-action window-action-minimize"
title="Minimize"><span>Minimize</span></a></li>
    <li class="window-action-wrapper window-action-wrapper-
maximize"><a href="#" class="window-action window-action-
maximize" title="Maximize"><span>Maximize</span></a></li>
    <li class="window-action-wrapper window-action-wrapper-
restore"><a href="#" class="window-action window-action-
restore" title="Restore"><span>Restore</span></a></li>
    <li class="window-action-wrapper window-action-wrapper-
close"><a href="#" class="window-action window-action-close"
title="Close"><span>Close</span></a></li>
  </ul>
</div>
```

This is a simple example with a series of buttons with their action displayed on them. Add this HTML to the `index.html` right after the opening **body** tag (and before the opening `main` tag). Next, we need some CSS. Add the following to `style.css`:

```
.window-bar {
  position: fixed;
  top: 0;
  left: 0;
  right: 0;
  padding: 15px;
  background: #e3e3e3;
}

.window-actions {
  display: flex;
  list-style: none;
  margin: 0;
  padding: 0;
  float: right;
}

.window-action-wrapper {
  display: flex;
  align-items: center;
  flex: 1;
  padding: 0 8px;
  order: 1;
}

.window-action-wrapper-restore {
  display: none;
}

.window-action {
  padding: 8px;
  border-radius: 100%;
  opacity: 0.8;
  transition: 0.25s opacity, 0.5s box-shadow;
}

.window-action:hover {
  opacity: 1;
  box-shadow: 0 1px 2px rgba(0, 0, 0, 0.1);
}

.window-action span {
  display: none;
}

.window-action-minimize {
  background: #fcd000;
}
```

```
.window-action-maximize,
.window-action-restore {
  background: #00fc65;
}

.window-action-close {
  background: #fc0000;
}

main {
  margin-top: 46px;
}
```

Here's the result:

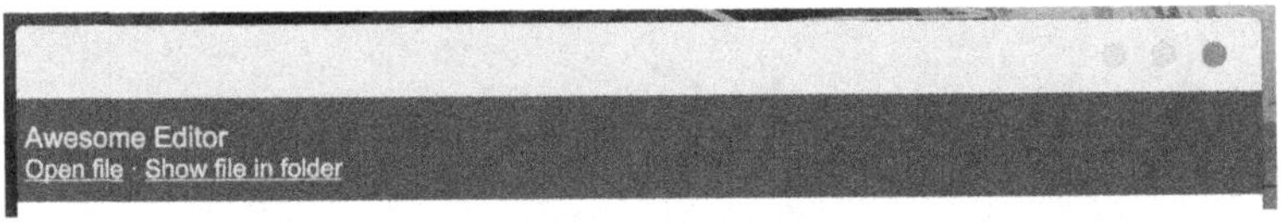

In the real world, we'd put in more effort, designing some actual icons. What we have are three circular buttons varying in color, placed in the top right corner of the app, where the window controls are expected to be on Windows. There's some interesting CSS here. Specifically, flexbox (the CSS flexible box layout module) is used to lay out the buttons.

What about Mac OS X? Well, if you've added `platform-mac` to the <body>, as shown earlier, you just need some extra CSS:

```
.platform-mac .window-actions {
  float: left;
}

.platform-mac .window-action-wrapper-close {
  order: 0;
}
```

We've placed the buttons in the top left corner and re-ordered them. Thanks to the **Flexbox (CSS Flexible Box Layout Module)**, the close button is now first (from the left), as you'd expect in a Mac app. Precisely, `.window-action-wrapper-close` has `order: 0`, whereas the rest of the `.window-action-wrappers` have `order: 1`. Since they have the same value, they're then ordered among themselves as they are in the HTML source.

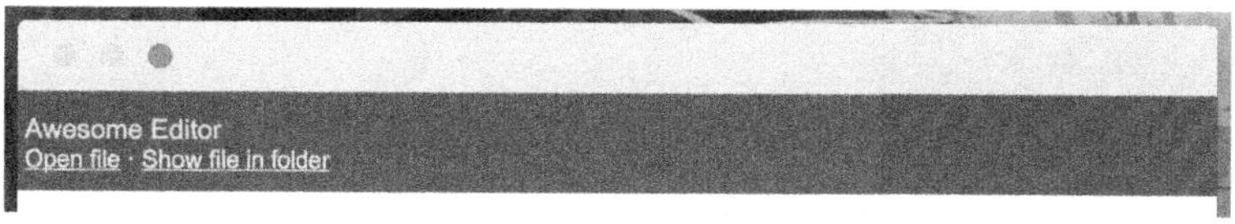

We now need to handle what happens when the buttons are clicked. We'll do this by catching clicks on any of the anchors, and then perform the desired action based on which one is clicked. The `BrowserWindow` has a method for each action, but the only issue is that our `mainWindow` belongs in the main process. Therefore, we'll need to bind the event handlers in `rendererScript.js`, inform the main process via IPC, and then call the appropriate method in the main script. Here's what we'll need in `index.js`:

```
const ipcRenderer = require('electron').ipcRenderer;

// ...

var forEach = function(selector, callback){
    return
[].forEach.call(document.querySelectorAll(selector),
callback);
};

var actions = ['minimize', 'maximize', 'restore', 'close'];

forEach('.window-action', (windowAction) => {
    windowAction.onclick = (e) => {
        actions.forEach((actionName) => {
            var classNameSegment = actionName;
            if(windowAction.classList.contains('window-
action-' + classNameSegment)){
                ipcRenderer.send('main-window',
classNameSegment);
            }
        });
    };
});
```

We bind click handlers to each `.window-action` and once clicked, send a `main-window` IPC event containing one of the following: `minimize`, `maximize`, `restore`, or `close`. To handle this in the main script, all you need is this:

```
const ipcMain = electron.ipcMain;

// ...

ipcMain.on('main-window', (event, windowActionName) => {
  if(windowActionName === 'restore'){
    mainWindow.unmaximize();
  }
  else {
    mainWindow[windowActionName]();
  }
});
```

This can be placed as early in the script as you'd like. We're mapping the `windowActionName` argument to a method of the `mainWindow`, such as `mainWindow.minimize`, `mainWindow.maximize`, `mainWindow.close`, and strangely `mainWindow.unmaximize`, not `mainWindow.restore`.

Speaking of restoring, earlier in this chapter we hid the restore button in our CSS with `display: none`. We need to show that, but only when the window is maximized. Thankfully, the `BrowserWindow` API provides `maximize` and `unmaximize` events.

Since all window management must be done in the main process, we need to use IPC again. All we have to update in `main.js` is the `ready` event callback:

```
app.on('ready', () => {
  mainWindow = new BrowserWindow({
    width: 800,
    height: 600,
    frame: false
  });
  mainWindow.loadURL('file://' + __dirname + '/index.html');

  mainWindow.on('maximize', () => {
    mainWindow.webContents.send('maximized');
  });
  mainWindow.on('unmaximize', () => {
    mainWindow.webContents.send('restored');
  });
});
```

As you can see above, we're catching these events and sending either `maximized` or `restored` events over to the renderer script. Adding the following to `index.js` will catch these events on the other side:

```
ipcRenderer.on('maximized', () => {
    document.body.classList.add('window--is-maximized');
});

ipcRenderer.on('restored', () => {
    document.body.classList.remove('window--is-maximized');
});
```

Since we now have a `window--is-maximized` class on the <body>, we can easily toggle the visibility of the maximize and restore buttons in `style.css`:

```
.window-action-wrapper-restore,
.window--is-maximized .window-action-wrapper-maximize {
  display: none;
}

.window--is-maximized .window-action-wrapper-restore {
  display: flex;
}
```

This is just the tip of the iceberg when it comes to the `BrowserWindow` API.

Draggability

You may have noticed that our example no longer has a bar that we can click and drag to move the window around. Amazingly, this can be handled via CSS in Electron. All you need is `-webkit-app-region`:

```
.window-bar {
  -webkit-app-region: drag;
}

.window-action {
  -webkit-app-region: no-drag;
}
```

So here we make the `.window-bar` draggable, but we must make sure that it's disabled for any inner elements that are clickable. One small thing to note is that if there is any text inside the draggable element, it's best to disable text selection via `user-select: none;`.

Uh oh

Yes, there's a catch. On Mac OS X, windows typically have a head and a body. Take a look at the Finder windows for example. While the window is not focused, you can click something in the header. If you were to click something in the body while the window is blurred, nothing happens. This is not a bug, it is intended behavior. It's a platform expectation.

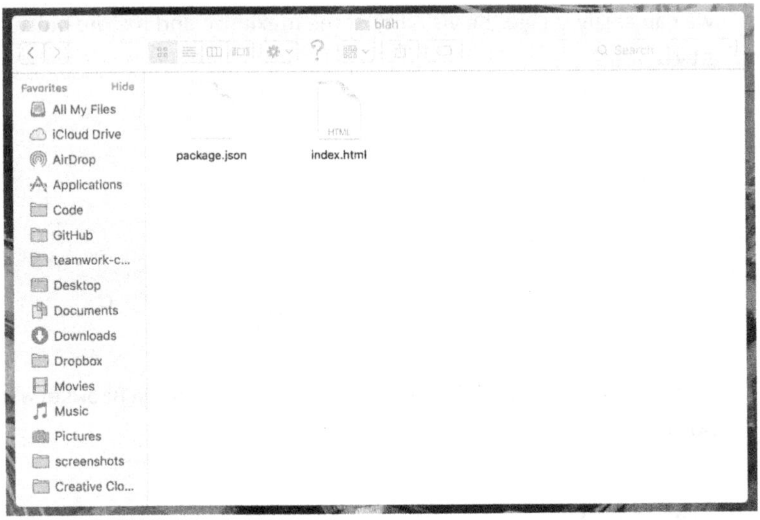

If you think about Chrome, or Chromium in our case, the head is where the browser controls are. Whereas the body of the window consists solely of the Webpage. Therefore, as of right now, our window has no header and the app is contained within the body. This is why custom HTML window controls should not be implemented on Mac OS X.

If you go with a custom frame for your Mac app, two clicks are required to click a window control when your app is blurred. The first click focuses your app. The second click triggers the click event on the element. Hovering over them won't result in the hover styles being applied. This is terribly frustrating for the user, and unfortunately, a common pitfall a lot of developers fall into. Please don't do it.

Note: there is a bug in Chromium which means that clicks and hover styles can be triggered on a blurred window. This only occurs when the user moves their cursor quickly, from outside the bounds of the window, to somewhere over it. This is scheduled to be fixed.

A nice workaround

The Electron team has your back though. Instead of specifying `frame: false` when initializing the window, passing `titleBarStyle: 'hidden'` provides the best of both worlds. What it does is hide the native frame, but overlays native window controls over your app.

There are no problems when your window is blurred, but your app can still be dragged around if clicked anywhere along where the title bar used to be. Now you no longer need any custom HTML or styles (including `-webkit-app-region`) in your Mac app.

Linux

We don't believe custom frames are worth it for Linux. You've seen what it takes to detect which distribution and version the user is currently running. Ideally, you'd want to fit in with the current platform. You want your app to feel at home, even if you're using a custom frame to allow for a bit of customization. Each distribution and version can have a window style that you need to mimic. Not only is this tedious, but you'll also need to maintain these styles. If a new version of a certain distribution changes its GUI, then you should follow suit, because it's not worth it. Using a native frame means that it's always up to date and in-sync with the operating system. It's the more reliable option, it's less work, and native frames on Linux don't look too bad anyway.

Summary

Now you know which platform users are on and you can make your app feel more at home on their desktops. All of the code is available at **github.com/adam-lynch/developing-an-electron-edge/tree/master/06-PlatformDetectionAndCustomFrames**. Feel free to take the `platform.js` module described. Use it and build on top of it. Platform detection will prove particularly useful when dealing with some of the platform-specific desktop integrations Electron provides you with, which is covered in the next chapter. We will also take a close look at frames (native, HTML, and hybrid), along with a peek at what the `BrowserWindow` API has to offer.

Desktop Integrations 7

You may be wondering what else you can do with Electron that you can't do with a standard Web app? Well, a lot actually. Between what Node offers, and Electron's own APIs, you can integrate your app tightly with the desktop environment, which we will cover in this chapter.

We'll start by examining how to use native notifications and end with creating system dialogs and file pickers. We'll go through each and every possible custom action, menu, and more, which can be applied to your app's icon in the taskbar or dock. We'll discover how to show a progress bar and a badge count, and much more. As you'll soon see, you can also control the tray and menubar icons, their menus, and balloon notifications as well. We will even cover how to create Unity launcher shortcuts, bind global hotkeys, set your app to automatically launch at startup, open URLs in the machine's default browser, and open files with the default associated app.

If you're not convinced that desktop apps bring a lot to the table, or if you're not sure they're worth the effort, you will be by the end of this chapter.

Special paths

Let's take a look at the APIs. Operating systems afford native APIs to desktop apps for integrating into the desktop environment. Electron provides its own APIs, which allow you to tap into those native APIs, just like regular desktop apps. This allows you to add items to native menus, show notifications and dialogs, and so on.

One thing we'll cover first is the special paths, or important directories and files, to be aware of such as the user's home directory. This directory may vary from operating system to operating system, and the user might even be able to change its location themselves. That's why Electron's app.getPath is essential:

```
const app = require('electron').app;
var homeDirectory = app.getPath('home');
```

Passing an associated name, home in this case, will result in the path string being returned. The other possible names include:

- appData - Per-user application data directory, which by default points to:
  - %APPDATA% on Windows, typically %USERPROFILE%\AppData, which itself expands to C:\Users\<username>\AppData\.
  - $XDG_CONFIG_HOME or ~/.config on Linux.
  - ~/Library/Application Support on OS X.
- userData - The directory for storing your app's configuration files, which by default is the appData directory appended with your app's name.
- temp - Temporary directory. Typically %LOCALAPPDATA% (C:\Users \<username>\AppData\Local\Temp) on Windows, for example.
- desktop - The current user's Desktop directory.
- documents - Directory for a user's "My Documents."
- downloads - Directory for a user's downloads.
- music - Directory for a user's music.
- pictures - Directory for a user's pictures.
- videos - Directory for a user's videos.
- exe - Path to the current executable file. Note: app.getAppPath would return the path to the current application directory.

You should never reference any of these paths directly, but should always use app.getPath. It's possible to override any one of these to point somewhere else with app.setPath. For example:

```
const app = require('electron').app;
try {
  app.setPath('home', 'C:\temporary-home');
}
catch (e) {
```

```
    // handle the error
  }
```

Notice the `try` - `catch`. If there's any failure, an `Error` will be thrown, so it's better to be safe than sorry. Note: `app.getPath` will also throw an error on failure.

Be aware, if you want to change where Web pages' cookies and caches are stored, you must override the `userData` path *before* the `ready` event of the `app` module is emitted.

Opening files with your app

```
const app = require('electron').app;
app.on('open-file', (event, filePath) => {
  event.preventDefault();
  console.log('User tried to open ' + filePath);
});
```

You're familiar with the `open-file` event as we used it in our real world example in an earlier chapter. It's fired when a file was dropped on the dock icon or a document in the "recent documents" dock menu list was clicked. We showed you how you should handle the event, whether your app is running or it isn't. We've actually found this event to be a **little unreliable** when Electron apps aren't running though. This has been confirmed with the Electron developers and we've learned that Electron is just passing on information Mac OS X gives it. So the problem is on the operating system side of things. This could be resolved by the time you're reading this book, but you've been warned.

`open-file` isn't support on Windows, but the file path can be parsed from `process.argv` in your main process:

```
if(process.argv.length > 1){
  filePath = process.argv[1];
  // do something with it :)
}
```

`process.argv` is an array, whose first element is always the absolute path of the app itself. If the app was opened with a file, there will be a second element that is the absolute path to the file. This only applies to your `.exe`. During development, your unpacked app is started differently with different arguments.

Detecting production or development

So we need to take this file path into account if the code is running in "production", or as a packaged app. This is a condition that will come up again and again, so let's figure it out. When running the packaged app, the packaged app is run. That's obvious. During development, however, it's actually the (prebuilt) Electron app that's run (with your code). So you can check if you're in development or production by checking the current app name:

```
if(app.getName() !== 'Electron' && process.argv.length > 1){
  filePath = process.argv[1];
  // do something with it :)
}
```

User tasks (Windows)

This JumpList (as Microsoft calls it) can only contain tasks. It is recommended that these are the commands in your app that a user is most likely to use, and they should remain static, regardless of the state of your app.

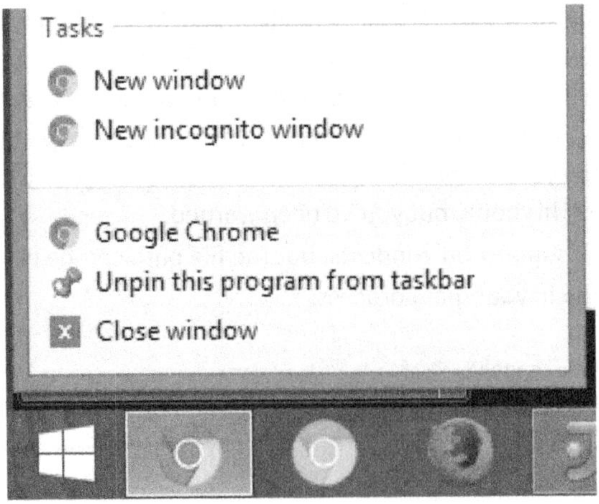

All tasks must be set at once by passing an array of tasks to `app.setUserTasks`:

```
app.setUserTasks([{
  title: 'Hello world',
```

```
    arguments: '--hello-world',
    program: process.execPath
  }, {
    title: 'Another task',
    program: process.execPath,
    arguments: '--another'
  }]);
```

As you can see, you need to supply a `title` for the label, the program that should be opened (`process.execPath` is the path to the current app on Windows), and the arguments that will be passed to it. As you might have guessed, clicking a task will open the given program (likely a new instance of your app) with the given arguments. Well, the argument. Ignore how the property is called `arguments`, since it will fail if you give more than one.

Note: tasks won't show during the development, only when running your `.exe`.

How do you know if the new instance was opened by an action? Again, it's `process.argv`. Let's extend the snippet from earlier to accept the task arguments:

```
const platform = require('./platform.js');

var taskCallbacks = {
  '--hello-world': () => {
    // so something
  },
  '--another': () => {
    // so something else
  }
}

if(process.argv.length > 1) {
  if(platform.isWindows && process.argv[1].indexOf('--') ===
0) {
    var callback = taskCallbacks[process.argv[1]];
    if(typeof callback === 'function'){
      callback();
    }
  }
  else {
    filePath = process.argv[1];
    // do something with it :)
  }
}
```

If `process.argv` contains multiple elements, check if the second element is a flag and that you're currently running on Windows. If so, and the flag is associated with a task, then handle it. If not, the argument must be a path of a file the app was opened with. This is a good start.

The tasks created above wouldn't have an icon. This can be set with an `iconPath` property. To show the icon of the current app, you can pass `process.execPath` again. If not, pass an absolute path, which can be an arbitrary resource file that contains an icon. There's also the `iconIndex` property, which is the index of the icon in the icon file that should be used. If you're using `iconPath`, make sure to use this property, and if you are unsure, pass `0`.

If given, the `description` property is used as the text of a tooltip shown when the user hovers over the task. A fully loaded task might look something like this:

```
app.setUserTasks([{
  title: 'Hello world',
  description: 'This is shown in a tooltip',
  arguments: '--hello-world',
  program: process.execPath,
  iconPath: process.execPath,
  iconIndex: 0
}]);
```

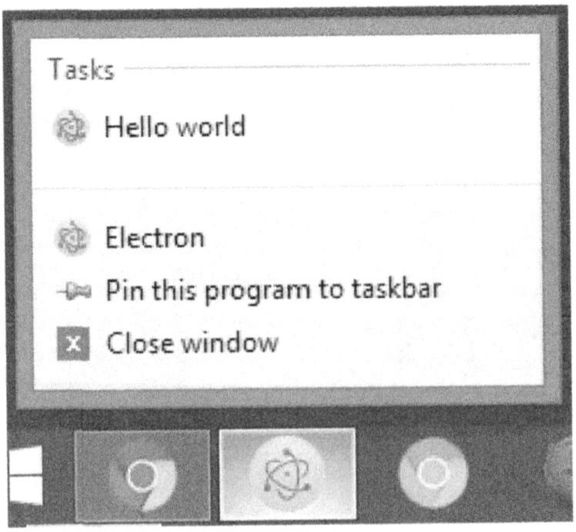

If you want to remove all tasks, you need to call `app.setUserTasks([])`.

Custom dock menu (Mac OS X)

You can also add your own items to the Mac OS X dock menu for your app.

```
const electron = require('electron');
const app = electron.app;
const Menu = electron.Menu;

var menu = Menu.buildFromTemplate([
  { label: 'Basic example', click: () => { /* do something
*/ } },
  { label: 'Nested', submenu: [
    { label: 'One', click: () => { /* do something */ } },
    { label: 'Two', click: () => { /* do something */ } }
  ]}
]);
app.dock.setMenu(menu);
```

Just like `setUserTasks`, `Menu.buildFromTemplate` accepts an array of objects. Each object has a `label` and either a `click` function or a `submenu` array of objects, each containing their own `label` and `click` callback.

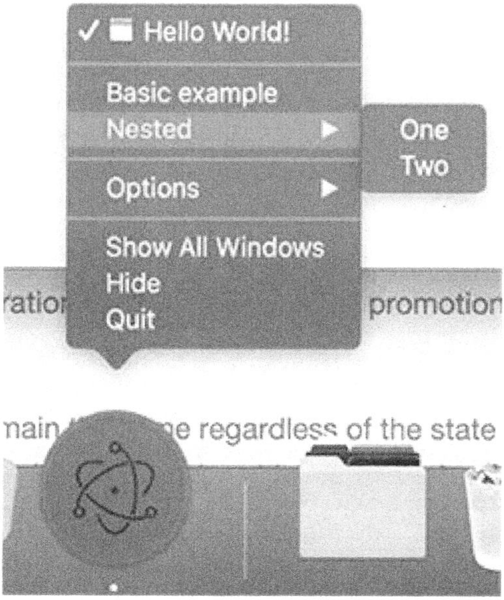

Unity launcher shortcuts (Linux)

It's also possible to do something similar in Unity. What you need to do is create a `.desktop` file.

Here's a full example from the **Ubuntu documentation** on the topic:

```
[Desktop Entry]
Version=1.0
Type=Application
Name=Audacious
GenericName=Music Player
Comment=Listen to music
Icon=audacious
Categories=AudioVideo;Audio;Player;GTK;

Exec=audacious %U

TryExec=audacious

Terminal=false

MimeType=application/ogg;application/x-cue;application/x-
ogg;application/xspf+xml;audio/midi;audio/mp3;audio/
mpeg;audio/mpegurl;audio/ogg;audio/prs.sid;audio/x-
flac;audio/x-it;audio/x-mod;audio/x-mp3;audio/x-mpeg;audio/x-
mpegurl;audio/x-ms-wma;audio/x-musepack;audio/x-s3m;audio/x-
```

```
scpls;audio/x-stm;audio/x-vorbis+ogg;audio/x-wav;audio/x-
xm;x-content/audio-cdda;

Actions=PlayPause;Next;Previous

[Desktop Action PlayPause]
Name=Play-Pause
Exec=audacious -t
OnlyShowIn=Unity;

[Desktop Action Next]
Name=Next
Exec=audacious -f
OnlyShowIn=Unity;

[Desktop Action Previous]
Name=Previous
Exec=audacious -r
OnlyShowIn=Unity;
```

Similarly to Windows, clicking an action will trigger a command with arguments.

Thumbnail toolbars (Windows 7+)

When hovering over a running app in the Windows taskbar, a popup appears above it containing the app's little version of the main window.

You can add up to seven buttons along the bottom of this popup. Windows Media Player shows previous, play or pause, and next buttons there. The `setThumbarButtons` method to set these isn't part of the `app` API, but the `BrowserWindow` one:

```
const BrowserWindow = require('electron').BrowserWindow;
const path = require('path');

var mainWindow = new BrowserWindow({
  // ...
});

mainWindow.setThumbarButtons([
  {
    icon: 'C:\\Users\\Username\\Desktop\\example.png',
    click: () => {
      console.log("Example button clicked");
    }
  },
  {
    tooltip: "Another example",
    icon: path.resolve('anotherExample.png'),
    flags:['dismissonclick'],
    click: () => {
      console.log("Another example button clicked.");
    }
  }
]);
```

You need to supply an absolute path `icon`, a `click` handler, and you can optionally give a string `tooltip` and or an array of `flags`. The values allowed in the `flags` array are as follows:

- `enabled`
- `disabled`
- `dismissonclick` - Hide the popover when the button is clicked.
- `nobackground` - Do not draw a button border.
- `hidden`
- `noninteractive` - The button is enabled but isn't interactive. This is intended to indicate something to the user.

If ommitted, `enabled` is the default.

If you want to edit any of these buttons afterward, you unfortunately need to set the entire array again. To remove them, use an empty array.

Represented file of window (Mac OS X)

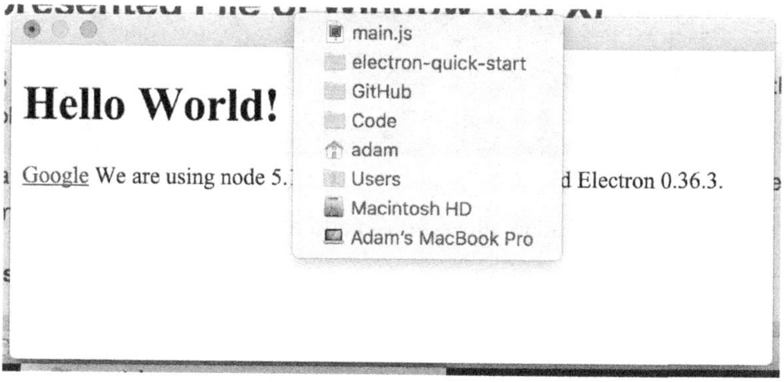

We've seen how to achieve this when creating our Markdown editor earlier, with `mainWindow.setRepresentedFilename`, but as well as that, you can also set the state of a window to indicate that the represented file has been modified:

```
mainWindow.setDocumentEdited(true);
```

Progress bar in taskbar

It's possible to indicate progress in the dock or taskbar icon.

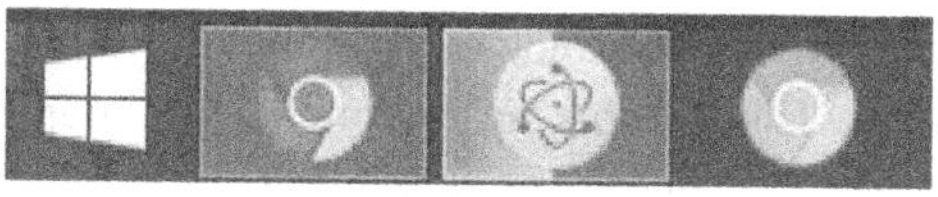

Each platform shows this in their own way, but the API is the same:

```
mainWindow.setProgressBar(0.5);
```

This is supported by Windows, Mac OS X, and some Linux distributions, including Unity.

Badge counts (Mac OS X)

`app.dock.setBadge` allows you to add a badge to the dock icon on Mac OS X.

```
const app = require('electron').app;

app.dock.setBadge('4');
app.dock.setBadge('.');
app.dock.setBadge(' ');
app.dock.setBadge('');
```

As you can see, you aren't limited to showing numbers. For example, you can pass a space if you just want an empty badge. To get the current badge value, call `app.dock.getBadge`.

Even more dock icon actions (Mac OS X)

If you're a Mac user, you've seen an app's dock icon bounce. Typically this happens if you try to open the app while it's already in the process of launching. You can programmatically trigger this bounce if you like, through `app.dock.bounce`. This accepts an optional type parameter that can either be `critical` or `informational`, which is the default.

If the type is `informational`, the app icon will bounce for one second, or until the app becomes active or focused if `critical` is passed.

It will return an ID (a bit like `setTimeout` or `setInterval`), which you can use to stop the bouncing by passing it to `app.dock.cancel-`

Bounce. One thing to note is that even though an informational bounce only lasts for one second, the request remains until the app is active or focused. Therefore, if you want your app to bounce three times for example, you need to do something like this:

```
var bounceAndCancel = function(callback){
  var bounceID = app.dock.bounce();
  setTimeout(function(){
    app.dock.cancelBounce(bounceID);

    // if a callback was given
    if(typeof callback === 'function'){
      callback();
    }
  }, 1000);
};

bounceAndCancel(function(){
  bounceAndCancel(bounceAndCancel);
});
```

So app.dock.bounce is only called again once the previous bounce is cancelled.

As well as bouncing, app facilitates hiding, showing, and changing the dock icon via app.dock.hide, app.dock.show, and app.dock.setIcon respectively.

Showing definitions (Mac OS X)

```
mainWindow.showDefinitionForSelection()
```

That will show the native definition popover for the text currently selected by the user:

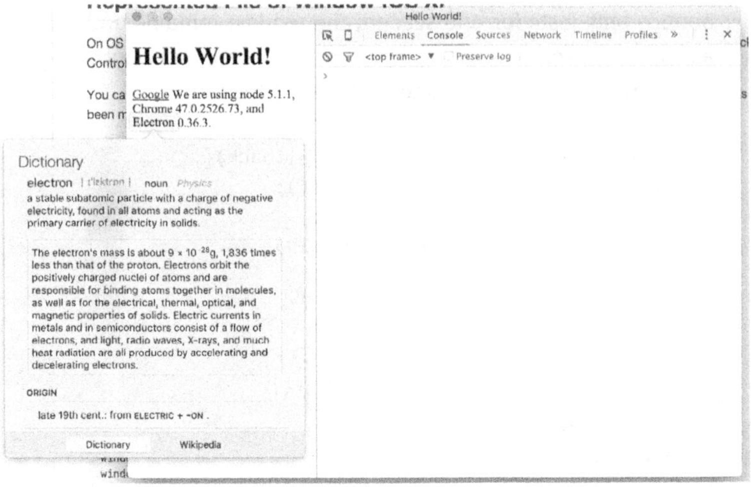

Global shortcuts

Electron allows you to bind keyboard shortcuts for your app that are fired even when the app isn't focused. That's nice. You could bind shortcuts to media keys for controlling music playback, or another shortcut might bring your app to the front with its a particular section open.

```
const electron = require('electron');
const globalShortcut = electron.globalShortcut;
```

A shortcut can be registered with the `globalShortcut.register` that accepts a key combination (such as `Ctrl`+V) and a callback that is called when the key combination is pressed. This returns a Boolean indicating whether or not the registration was successful. If it wasn't, it's properly due to an invalid key combination. You can also check if a key combination is already registered by passing it `globalShortcut.isRegistered`, which returns a Boolean.

Our options

A key combination can have multiple modifiers and key codes, joined together by plus symbols. The supported key codes are as follows:

- `0` to `9`.
- `A` to `Z`.
- `F1` to `F24`.
- Punctuation keys including `~`, `!`, `@`, `#`, `$`, etc.
- `Plus`.
- `Space`.
- `Backspace`.
- `Delete`.
- `Insert`.
- `Return` or `Enter` (which is just an alias).
- `Up`, `Down`, `Left`, and `Right`.
- `Home` and `End`.
- `PageUp` and `PageDown`.
- `Escape` (or `Esc` for short).
- `VolumeUp`, `VolumeDown`, and `VolumeMute`.
- `MediaNextTrack`, `MediaPreviousTrack`, `MediaStop`, and `MediaPlayPause`.

Then there are the modifiers that can be used in combination with key codes:

- `Command` (or `Cmd` for short).
- `Control` (or `Ctrl` for short).
- `CommandOrControl` (or `CmdOrCtrl` for short).
- `Alt`.
- `Shift`.
- `Super`.

`Command` does nothing on Windows or Linux because they don't have that key, but `CommandOrControl` is a handy one. It's there for cases like binding to `Ctrl+Shift+V` on Windows and Linux, but `Command+V` on Mac OS X.

`Super` is similar. On Windows and Linux, it is mapped to the Windows key, but the command key on Mac.

An example

Make sure only to use this API in your main process, and after the app's `ready` event is emitted.

```
const electron = require('electron');
const app = electron.app;
const globalShortcut = electron.globalShortcut;

app.on('ready', () => {
  var isRegistered = globalShortcut.register('Ctrl+V', () =>
{
    // ctrl+v is pressed
  });

  if (!isRegistered) {
    // Registration failed
  }
});
```

Unregistering

You can call `globalShortcut.unregister` passing a certain key combination to unbind it, or call `globalShortcut.unregisterAll` to remove all global keyboard shortcuts.

Shortcut clashes

Your shortcut bindings can prevent them from working for other apps and vice versa. If you want to detect when your registration of a shortcut fails, you have two options. You can either check the return value of `globalShortcut.register` as shown in the last example, or use `globalShortcut.isRegistered`, passing it your combination:

```
var isRegistered = globalShortcut.isRegistered('Ctrl+V');
```

System dialogs

You might notice that you can't use `alert` or `confirm` in your main process as they're not defined. You shouldn't do that anyway as a browser-style alert would look strange in a desktop app. What you want is native dialogs. There's an API for that:

```
const dialog = require('electron').dialog;
```

The following is the equivalent of `alert`:

```
dialog.showMessageBox({
  message: 'ERROR',
  buttons: []
});
```

It will show a system dialog with your message and an OK button (which just closes the dialog).

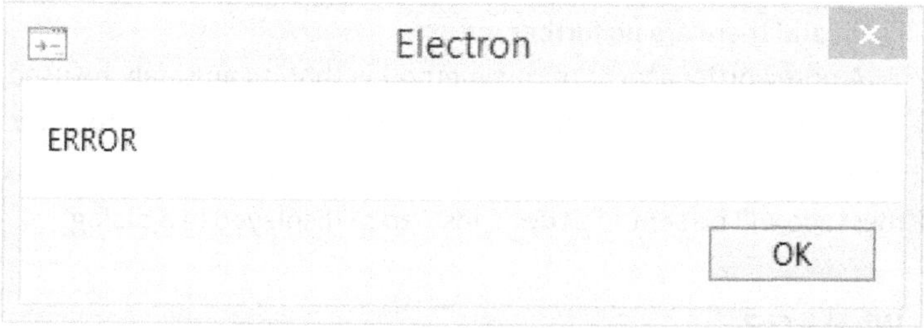

Let's make a `confirm` dialog. All we're missing is two buttons and the ability to handle them. You can add as many buttons as you'd like, by adding strings to the `buttons` array for the buttons' text. You can also pass a callback, which is called with the index of the clicked button.

```
dialog.showMessageBox({
  message: 'ERROR',
  buttons: ['OK', 'Cancel']
}, (indexOfButton) () => {
  if(indexOfButton === 0){
    // "OK" was clicked
  }
  else {
    // "Cancel" was clicked
  }
});
```

If the dialog is closed by some other means other than clicking a button, then the callback is called too. If you have a "Cancel" or "No" button, then that ID is used. If not, then `0` is used, and the index of your buttons start at `1`.

Note: the buttons are shown in reverse order.

You can pass a window object as an optional first argument if you'd like. There are a few other options at your disposal, including a `detail` string for an extra line of text, `title` for the title of the dialog, and a `type` property that can be either `"none"`, `"info"`, `"error"`, `"question"` or `"warning"`. On Windows, `"question"` is just shown as `"info"`, but you can workaround that with the `icon` option.

Uh oh!

There's also `dialog.showErrorBox(title, content)` for showing a native dialog specifically for error messages. Those arguments must be given and there are no further options.

A noteworthy aspect of this method is that it can safely be used anywhere, even before the app's `ready` event is fired. That's handy for notifying the user of fatal errors early. If called before `ready` on Linux, the message will be sent to `stderr` instead of displayed in a dialog.

Where to?

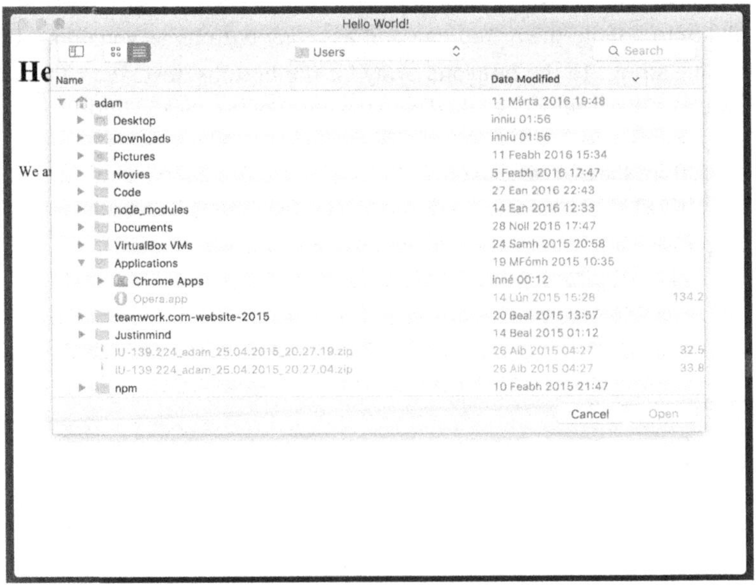

We saw how to open the file picker in an earlier chapter using the showOpenDialog method, but what about the opposition direction? dialog.showSaveDialog shows the typical operating system dialog for choosing a save location and a name for a file. You don't pass this method a file, this is just a way that the user can select a directory, and then you do whatever you want with that information.

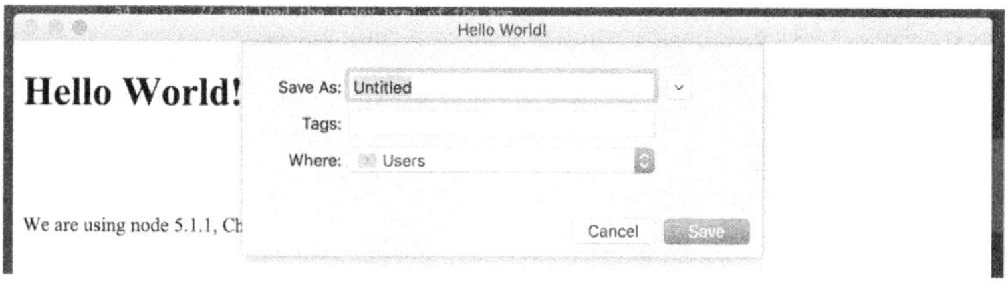


```
dialog.showSaveDialog(mainWindow, {
  title: 'A title',
  defaultPath: '/Users/',
  filters: []
}, (filePath) => {
  if(filePath){
    // Tada!
  }
});
```

All of the arguments there are optional. defaultPath and filters options are just like the showOpenDialog's ones. The callback acts the same too.

The Shell API

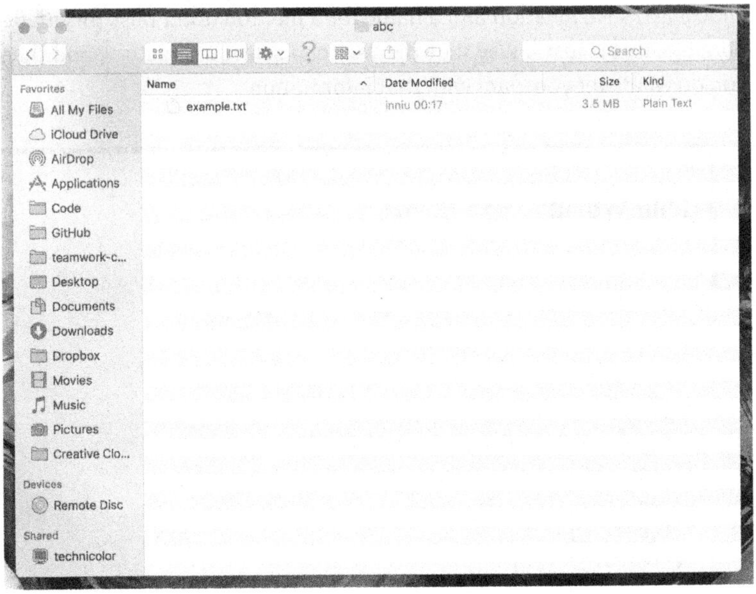

You might remember the "Shell" module from earlier when we used its `showItemInFolder` method to reveal the location of a Markdown file from our editor. As of right now, the Shell API contains a few other simple yet important methods for performing OS level actions on file paths or URLs. These methods call platform-specific methods within Chromium, which can differ a lot per platform. Couple that with discrepancies in the behavior of the system actions or programs being called, the outcome can be inconsistent. Most of the methods don't have return values so it's best to manually test each platform yourself to be safe. This module can be used in either the main process or in the renderer processes.

Opening a resource

To open an arbitrary directory, you can pass the path to `shell.openItem`:

```
var shell = require('electron').shell;
shell.openItem('/Users/adam/Desktop/abc');
```

Actually, `shell.openItem` will open a path to *any* file in the default program associated with the file's type. Directory paths open in your file browser, MP3s open in your default music player, and text files are opened in your favorite text editor.

This method can open a lot of doors, but be careful. When there is no program associated with the given file extension or file type, the result varies. Some platforms will do nothing, alhough some show a "The application can't be found" message or that there is no default program. Some even go as far as giving the user the choice of which application to open the file with.

Opening URLs

`shell.openExternal` is specifically for URLs. The following will open the given URL in the current user's default browser:

```
var shell = require('electron').shell;
shell.openExternal('http://www.example.com');
```

We advise *only* passing absolute URLs. This method is exceptional in that the browser opens even if a non-existent URL is passed. The browser will try to open the URL and show you the result as normal.

The only case where the browser isn't opened is when the method is called with something with strange characters or something that doesn't pass the basic validation Chromium does before passing the URL off to the default browser. This validation is different per platform, so some URLs may not work on every platform.

The following bug has been fixed, but serves as a good example. Let's suppose the URL was provided to the user and they accidentally hit the backslash key next to the return key when submitting your form. Let's say the user entered `http://www.example.com/index.html#abc\`, which if entered into Google Chrome or Apple's Safari's address bar, would show `http://www.example.com/index.html#abc` without a problem. Surprisingly then, (before the bug was patched) passing `http://www.example.com/index.html#abc\` to `shell.openExternal` works as expected on Windows, but does nothing on Mac OS X.

LINKS

By default, clicking an anchor in an Electron window will navigate the Electron window away from your app's page to wherever the link is pointing to. This is just like a link works in Google Chrome. This is almost never what you want for your desktop application, especially if the links are part of the content provided by the user. That's why this method is essential.

Since you might have the same problem in a Web browser, you first add `target="_blank"` to the anchor in question so it is opened in a new tab when clicked.

Note: no JavaScript needed.

In Electron, clicking the link opens a *new* Electron window. There are a few different ways to approach this, so I'll just keep it simple. Let's assume that all links with `target="_blank"` are external links, and all other links are ok for Electron to navigate to. A good example of this are links to other pages within your app.

```
var shell = require('electron').shell;

var isExternalLink = (element) => element.tagName === 'A' &&
element.target === '_blank';

var isInExternalLink = (element) => {
  parent = element.parentNode;
  while(parent && parent !== document.body) {
    if(isExternalLink(parent)) {
      return true;
    }
    parent = parent.parentNode;
  }
  return false;
};

var onClick = (e) => {
  if(isExternalLink(e.target) || isInExternalLink(e.target)){
    e.preventDefault();
    shell.openExternal(e.target.href);
  }
};

document.body.addEventListener('click', onClick, false);
```

This bit of JavaScript does the following:

- Catches all clicks, anywhere in the document.
- Ignores clicks where the target of the click isn't an anchor or isn't an element within an anchor, with `target="_blank"`.

- If an external link was clicked, then the default browser action is blocked and `shell.openExternal` is called with the target URL of the anchor.

If your app code is run in an Electron application as well as on the Web, then you can add checks to see which environment your app is currently running in, or simply don't attach the event handler at all when in the Web. Either way, you're letting the browser handle it as it normally would. Although, you may be attaching the event handler anyway for some extra custom handling.

If you want to be even stricter, you can set all anchors (without a `target` attribute) to open in a new tab by default by putting `<base target="_blank">` in your `<head>`. Then you can manually add `target="_self"` to any links you want to be followed in the current Electron window, like links to other pages within your application.

Another alternative is to not add a `target` attribute to anchors or a `<base>` element at all, but instead check if a link is external using the useful **`local-links` module** (from npm), which has an `isLocal` method.

Recycling and beeping

`shell.moveItemToTrash` makes it easy to move files to the system recycle bin or trash. It's exceptional, in that it does return a value; a Boolean denoting success or failure.

```
var shell = require('electron').shell;
isDeleted = shell.moveItemToTrash('/Users/adam/Desktop/abc');
if(isDeleted){
  shell.beep();
}
```

As you can see, we call `shell.beep` if the deletion was successful. This is the final method of the bunch, responsible for playing the system's beep sound.

Notifications

It's pretty easy to display native notifications to the user on any platform. You just need the one API. Even better, it's an API you might already know: the **HTML5 Notifications API**. It's as simple as this:

```
var notification = new Notification('Title of notification',
{
  body: 'Body of notification'
});
```

The notification is just like a system notification and will go in the operating system's notifications area if it has one.

You don't need to request permission from the user, like you would when using this API on the Web. Although if you do call `Notification.requestPermission`, it will always succeed, so it's safe to share re-use code or libraries.

Be aware, this only supports plaintext. If you want to use HTML or show compiled Markdown for example, then you'll need custom HTML notifications, but more about that later.

Ok, but what if you want to handle when the notification is clicked? Then you'll also need this:

```
notification.onclick = () => {
  // do something
};
```

You'll need to set `onclick` for each `Notification` instance.

Ok, it's not that simple. Each operating system and version will display the notification similarly, but there are noteworthy differences between platforms.

OS X

Notifications are truncated if they go over 256 bytes in size.

Linux

Notifications are sent underneath via `libnotify`. Any desktop environment that follows **Desktop Notifications Specification** is supported, including Cinnamon, Enlightenment, Unity, GNOME, and KDE.

Windows

Notifications on Windows are truncated to 250 characters and Microsoft recommends keeping them under 200 characters in length.

You can show an image in your Windows notifications by passing a file URL (to a local image):

```
var notification = new Notification('Icon!', {
  body: 'Body of notification',
  icon: 'file:///C:/Users/hello-world/Downloads/notification-
icon.png'
});
```

Passing an incorrect path won't stop the notification from displaying. It'll still show fine, just without the image. The same thing happens if you pass a HTTP or HTTPS URL.

A FEW EXTRA HOOPS TO JUMP THROUGH

On Windows 10, thankfully, none of the following applies. On Windows 8 (and 8.1), you need to create a shortcut to your app (with a Windows **Application User Model ID**.aspx)) in order for it to work.

These notifications technically aren't supported on Windows 7 or older, but if you need to support Windows 7, then you have two remaining options: custom HTML notifications or creating "balloons" with the Tray API, and we'll elaborate on that soon.

Back to Windows 8 for a minute. I bet you were thinking, "but how do I create a shortcut to my app?" This is actually a bit awkward. When talking about installers and automatic updates, you'll see that this is solved by using Squirrel.Windows. If you don't want automatic updates, or don't want an installer or different installer (like NSIS), then follow along to learn how to get notifications working.

If you're using an NSIS installer, you can script your installer to create the shortcut (with the app ID). That's not great, though, because it's only done once when your app is installed. If the shortcut is deleted at any time, the notifications are broken.

You need to create the shortcut programmatically. That way, you can create the shortcut even if it doesn't exist every time your app is opened. Also, since it's in your app code, it can change over time. You can tweak the code in an automatic update.

Unfortunately, Electron doesn't have a built-in method for creating shortcuts (unlike NW.js). You can write a native module to do this, as you'll see how in a later chapter, but that's a hassle (they can be a real pain on Windows). There are Node modules out there for creating shortcuts, but creating one with an app ID is the issue. Luckily, someone has forked one of these modules and added a method for adding the app ID (by bundling in an `.exe` to do it). This may be one person's little fork of a module, but it is the way to go, at least until Electron adds their own method.

```
npm install --save windows-shortcuts-appid
```

Now that you have the module, let's settle on an app ID. The app ID should follow the `com.squirrel.atom.Atom` format. What you need to do now is set the app's app ID using `app.setAppUserModelId`. Then, check if the shortcut already exists; if not, we'll create one and add the app ID to it.

```
const electron = require('electron');
const path     = require('path');
const fs       = require('fs');
const platform = require('./platform.js');
const ws       = require('windows-shortcuts-appid');

const app = electron.app;
const BrowserWindow = electron.BrowserWindow;

let mainWindow;

app.on('ready', () => {
  // Typical stuff
  mainWindow = new BrowserWindow({width: 800, height: 600});
  mainWindow.loadURL('file://' + __dirname + '/index.html');

  app.on('did-finish-load', () => {
    var appName = app.getName();
    // Only need to do this for Windows 8, in a packaged app
    if(appName !== 'Electron' && platform.isWindows8){
      var appId = "com.myCompany.myapp.MyApp";
      app.setAppUserModelId(appId);
```

```
        var shortcutPath = path.join(app.getPath('appData'),
"Roaming\\Microsoft\\Windows\\Start Menu\\Programs", appName
+ ".lnk");
        fs.exists(shortcutPath, (exists) => {
          if(exists) {
            // The shortcut already exists, no need to do
anything
            return;
          }

          // Create the shortcut
          ws.create(shortcutPath, process.execPath, (err) -> {
            if(err) throw err;

            // Add the app ID to the shortcut
            ws.addAppId(shortcutPath, appId, (err) -> {
              if(err) throw err;
              // Ready!
            });
          });
        });
      }
    });
  });
```

Now, notifications will work.

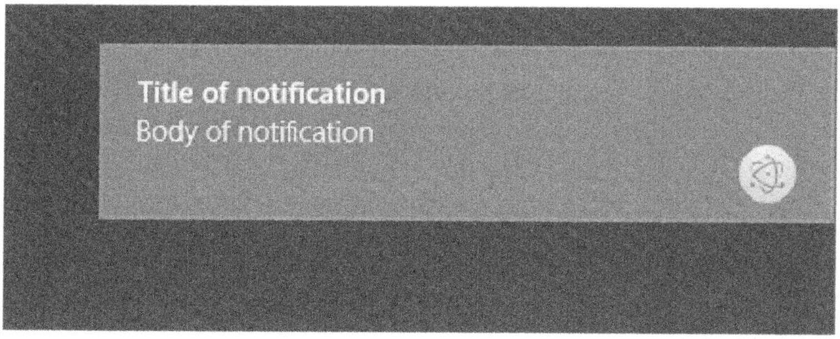

Yes!

Notice the path that is a location along the lines of `C:\Users\<username>\AppData\Roaming\...`.

Note: you'll never need higher permissions to write a file to `AppData`.

Metadata

You can easily link notifications to other things. For example, you may want to do something different on the page depending on the notification that is clicked. You can add any property you like onto the notification and check it later.

```
var notification = new Notification('Title of notification',
{
  body: 'Body of notification'
});

notificaton.itemId = 123;
notification.hello = 'world';

notification.onclick = function() {
  console.log(this.itemId); // 123
  console.log(this.hello); // world
};
```

Custom HTML notifications

If you really need to, you can create your own custom HTML notifications and design them however you like. Add ten images if you want (please don't). Remember, though, that each notification consumes its own amount of memory. There's also a bit of work involved. You'll need to manage how many images can be shown at one time, the timeouts, how they animate in, and making sure they work in mutli-screen setups. A lot of the work the operating system has already done for you. Plus, your custom notifications won't go in the native notifications area if the OS has one. It's best to only do this if you have to. We recommend an open source module that does all of this for you.

The Tray API

With this API, you can put an icon in the operating system's notification area.

```
const electron = require('electron');
const app = electron.app;
const Tray = electron.Tray;

var trayIcon = null;
```

```
app.on('ready', () => {
  trayIcon = new Tray('/path/to/icon.png');
});
```

Note: On Linux boxes that only have app indicator support, you have to install `libappindicator1` to make the tray icon work.

The `tray` icon emits `click`, `right-click`, and `double-click` events, but these aren't consistent across platforms, so it's best to always use a context menu. Let's give our tray icon a context menu and a tooltip while we're at it.

```
const electron = require('electron');
const app = electron.app;
const Menu = electron.Menu;
const Tray = electron.Tray;

var trayIcon = null;
app.on('ready', () => {
  trayIcon = new Tray('/path/to/icon.png');
  trayIcon.setToolTip('This is my application.');
  trayIcon.setContextMenu(Menu.buildFromTemplate([
    { label: 'Item1', type: 'radio', click: () => {} },
    { label: 'Item2', type: 'radio', checked: true, click:
() => {} }
  ]));
});
```

There you go. Pretty simple. Other useful methods include `trayIcon.destroy` and `trayIcon.setToolTip`.

Balloons

As alluded to previously, having a tray icon allows you to trigger Windows-XP style balloon notifications in the notification area on Windows.

```
trayIcon.displayBalloon({
  icon: 'path/to/icon.png',
  title: 'Head',
```

```
    content: 'Body'
  });
```

That's how you show a balloon. The `icon` property is optional; a system one will be used if it's omitted (as shown above). We can also listen for `balloon-show`, `balloon-click`, and `balloon-closed` events.

```
  trayIcon.on('balloon-show', () => {
    // Tada!
  });

  trayIcon.displayBalloon({
    icon: 'path/to/icon2.png',
    title: 'Head',
    content: 'Body'
  });
```

You might be wondering though, what's the point of these events if they're emitted when *any* balloon is shown, clicked, or closed? Well, as of right now, there's no way to identify a notification by tacking on your own ID or anything like that. Too bad.

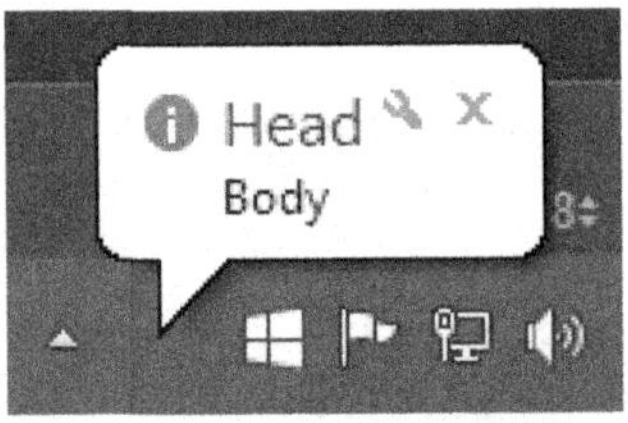

You can, however, have balloon notifications without the tray icon. When instatiating the Tray, pass `null` for the icon (`new Tray(null)`) and you'll have an empty entry in the notification area. It's a little weird though, because this is how it looks when you hover over it:

Let's be honest, these notifications aren't the prettiest. We recommend that you only use them if you really need to or if you have a compelling use case.

Automatically launching your app on startup

Wouldn't you like your app to open when the user logs onto their machine? Or at least give the user that option? Of course you would. This is surprisingly easy, because we created a little module called **node-auto-launch** at Teamwork.com for this exact purpose.

The module is of course available on npm: run `npm install --save auto-launch` to get it. First, you need to set up an AutoLaunch instance:

```
var AutoLaunch = require('auto-launch');
var myAutoLauncher = new AutoLaunch({
    name: 'My App Name',
    path: '/Applications/MyApp.app'
});
```

This instance comes with three methods that do exactly as is said on the tin: `myAutoLauncher.enable`, `myAutoLauncher.disable` and `myAutoLauncher.isEnabled`.

Simple, right? Well, this module was actually created with NW.js and Electron in mind so you don't even have to pass the `path` property at all. For Electron apps, the `path` will be inferred automatically. Magic.

For example, if you want to set the app to launch on boot, you might do the following:

```
const AutoLaunch = require('auto-launch');
var electronAutoLauncher = new AutoLaunch({
    name: 'My Electron App Name'
});

electronAutoLauncher.isEnabled((enabled) => {
    if(enabled){
        // It's already set!
        return;
    }

    electronAutoLauncher.enable((err) => {
        if(err){
            throw(err);
        }

        // Tada!
    });
});
```

Let's talk platforms

Relax, you should be safe enough. Windows, Mac, and Linux are supported. For Linux users, a `.desktop` file is created. This follows the **Desktop Entry Specification**, which both KDE and GNOME support.

Hidden mode

The constructor also accepts an `isHidden` Boolean property that is currently only supported on Mac OS X. When this property is `true`, your app will launch in hidden mode at login. This just means your app will run, but remain hidden on your desktop.

Be careful during development

If this code is run during development, the Electron app you installed via npm (used to run your app) will be launched every time you start up your machine. To avoid this, and only run this code in your packaged application, you can manually set an `isDev` variable (possibly in a build script) based on the production/development detection code we had earlier, or to be really safe you can check if `process.execPath` contains *any* of the following: `Electron.app`, `Electron Helper.app`, `Electron.exe`, or more. If it does contain a string like these examples, you don't want to run this code because it's not being run in your packaged app.

Summary

So there you have it. We've covered a wide range of integrations that are vital tools in the rich desktop application toolbox. You've also explored some of the intricacies involved in creating a complex cross-platform desktop app, like what it really takes to nail notifications, for example.

What's great is that these integrations are additional bonuses, on top of what Node.js and native modules allow you to do with Electron anyway.

When integrating as tightly as this into the desktop environment, platform detection has come in handy, allowing you to work around platform or version variances or incompatibilities. Similarly, you can now conditionally run code if your app is running from a "production" application or during development. This is key.

As you can see, you can do a whole lot more with an Electron app than you could ever do with a standard Web app. New apps are being created every day with increasingly interesting uses for these APIs. Go ahead, impress us.

Debugging 8

In the last few chapters you've learned a lot about developing a real Electron application and how to make use of native features to make it look like a real desktop application. Now it is time to talk about debugging. As soon as something doesn't work exactly the way you expect it to, you have a problem. If you run your application, during runtime it is a blackbox and you don't know exactly what happens inside. In this chapter you'll discover how to debug the various processes of your application.

Debugging is an essential and important part of developing. It is crucial to go through your application step-by-step if something doesn't work as it should. Debugging often reveals errors that would be very hard to find otherwise.

Different programming environments and languages provide very different tools for debugging, and often this is already built in the IDE.

Debugging JavaScript is a bit more complicated. The fact that it is interpreted at runtime and not compiled into some byte code representation makes it harder to debug during runtime. Luckily, the Chrome browser comes with a very good JavaScript debugging environment that you can use.

Renderer Processes

The Renderer processes are the ones you start from the main process. You usually load your HTML file over a `file://` URL, and a headless Chrome window displays the contents and runs all of the JavaScript code that is included. Regardless if you have enabled the `nodeIntegration` option, you can use Chrome's JavaScript debugger to directly step through your code.

To do this, you need to display the Developer Tools window for your renderer process. This can be done as follows (from the main process):

```
var mainWindow = new BrowserWindow({ width: 800, height:
600 });
mainWindow.loadURL('file://' + __dirname + '/index.html');

mainWindow.webContents.openDevTools();
```

When you run your application now, the Dev Tools window should automatically open. Per default, it is attached and displayed inside your renderer window, but you can also detach it by the button in the upper right side of the window.

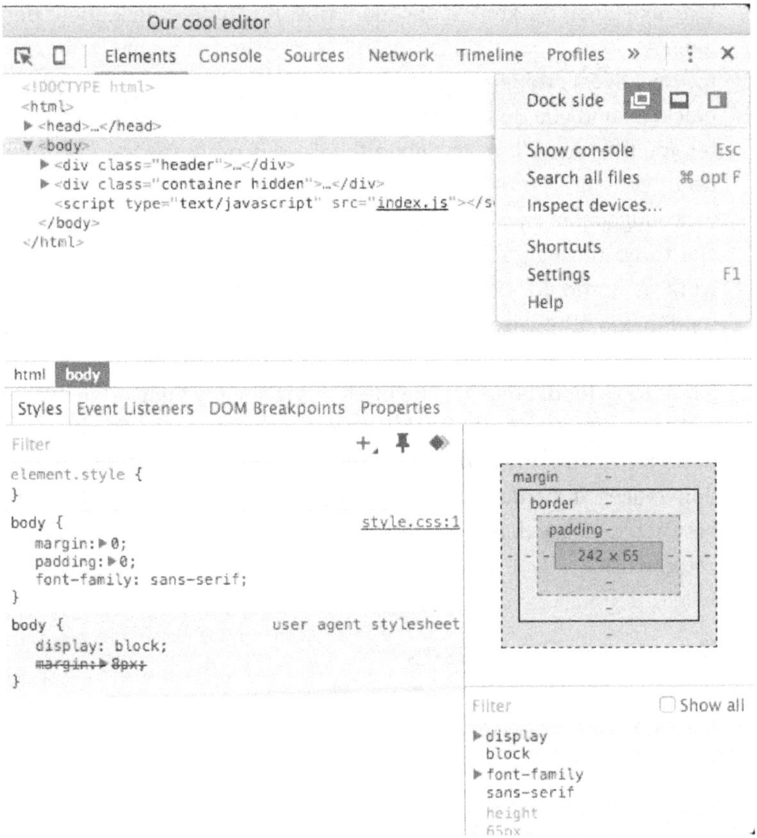

There are different tabs in the Developer Tools window that let you inspect various aspects of your application. Let's examine the most important ones here.

The "Elements" tab

In the "Elements" tab you'll find the DOM representation of your page and you can make changes to it. You can also inspect the applied CSS values for every element in the DOM. Also, you can directly insert new CSS properties and see how it will look in real-time.

The "Console" tab

The "Console" tab is very valuable. Not only do you see all of the standard output of the renderer's JavaScript code and possible errors, but you can also execute JavaScript code in the environment of the renderer process. To have access to certain variables in this console, the easiest thing to do is to just assign them to the `window` object:

```
var ipcRenderer = require('electron').ipcRenderer;
window.ipcRenderer = ipcRenderer;
```

(This only works if `nodeIntegration` is set to `true`, which is the default.)

Now you have access to the `ipcRenderer` module, which let's you execute actions in the `mainProcess`.

This is the code for the `main.js`:

```
const electron = require('electron');
const app = electron.app;
const BrowserWindow = electron.BrowserWindow;
const ipcMain = electron.ipcMain;

var mainWindow = null;

ipcMain.on('say-hello', (evt, arg) => {
  evt.returnValue = 'Hello ' + arg;
});

app.on('ready', () => {
  mainWindow = new BrowserWindow({ width: 800, height:
600 });
```

```
    mainWindow.loadURL('file://' + __dirname + '/index.html');
    mainWindow.webContents.openDevTools();
});
```

Let's run the application now and play around in the console!

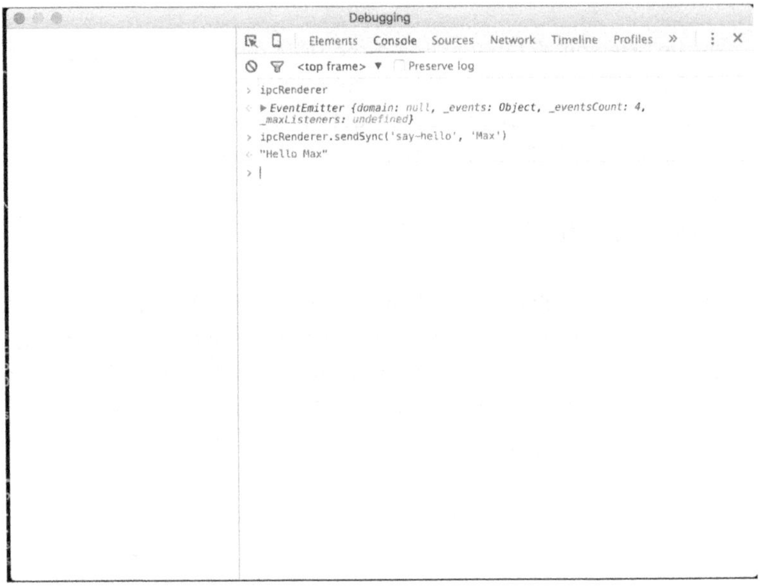

The "Console" tab is definitely one of the most important tools you have to debug your application and inspect it while running. You can also `console.log()` values to inspect them during runtime.

The "Sources" tab

The "Sources" tab is even more important for debugging. It shows us not only all the scripts that you've loaded, but it also let's you set breakpoints in them. If you've set a breakpoint, the application will stop as soon as it gets to the breakpoint in the source file and let's you manually step over/into the operations. It also let's you inspect all of the current set variables. This is a wonderful tool for debugging.

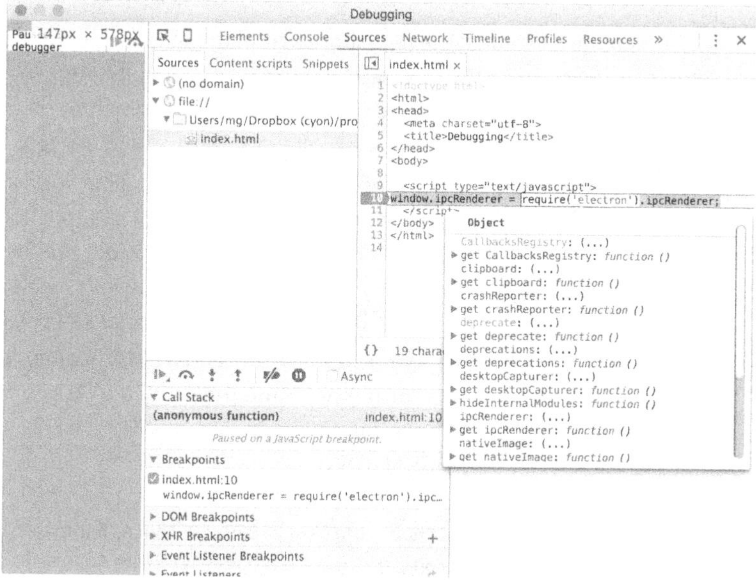

We encourage you to get to know the debugger. Consider setting up a little test application and just play around with it. Expect variables, step over/in/out, and just get to know this powerful tool.

The "Network" tab

The next tab is the "Network" tab. It contains detailed information for all of the network requests that happen inside your app. You can also see a timeline for all requests made and the total time it took to load all assets and display your page.

Let's add a few network requests to the previous example to test that out.

First, we love using Google's **Roboto font**. So please add the following lines to the end of your <head> of your `index.html` file:

```
<link href='https://fonts.googleapis.com/css?family=Roboto'
rel='stylesheet' type='text/css'>
<style type="text/css">
body {
  font-family: 'Roboto';
}
</style>
```

This will load the font directly from Google's servers so you can use it in your CSS.

Let's create a list of all the repositories from the **atom** organization on Github. To accomplish this you need to make use of Github's API. The API call specifically is **list-user-repositories**, and the documentation page shows that this can be used very easily. All you have to do is a GET `https://api.github.com/users/atom/repos` call. There is a small catch, though. Because the atom organization has a lot of repositories, you won't get all of them in the same response. You only get the first 30 ones (alphabetically).

They do have documentation on how you can **traverse API responses with pagination** and it's very clever. They send a `Link` header in the response, which gives links for the next, the previous, the last and the first page. It doesn't include the current one.

The `Link` header may look like this:

```
Link: <https://api.github.com/user/1089146/repos?page=3>;
rel="next", <https://api.github.com/user/1089146/repos?
page=7>; rel="last", <https://api.github.com/user/1089146/
repos?page=1>; rel="first", <https://api.github.com/user/
1089146/repos?page=1>; rel="prev"
```

This makes it easy. You just have to get the results from the next link until there is no more next link. Parsing this is not that trivial, but we know what the link should look like, so you can use a regular expression:

```
/<(https:\/\/api.github.com\/user\/[0-9]*\/repos\?page
\=[0-9]*)>; rel="next"/g
```

If you're not familiar with regular expressions, check out the following guide by Mozilla: **https://developer.mozilla.org/en-US/docs/Web/JavaScript/Guide/Regular_Expressions**

To fetch the data from the API use the **Fetch API**, which is **not yet supported** by many browsers, but luckily it is by Chrome.

Let's write some code:

```
<body>

  <ul id="repos">
  </ul>

  <script type="text/javascript">
var reposList = document.getElementById('repos');
```

```
var url = 'https://api.github.com/users/atom/repos';

fetchPage(url);

function fetchPage (url) {
  fetch(url)
    .then((response) => {
      var link = response.headers.get('Link');
      var regex = /<(https:\/\/api.github.com\/user\/[0-9]*\/
repos\?page\=[0-9]*)>; rel="next"/g;
      var matches = regex.exec(link);

      if (matches) {
        fetchPage(matches[1]);
      }

      return response.json();
    })
    .then((json) => {
      json.map((repo) => {
        var el = document.createElement('li');
        el.textContent = repo.name;
        reposList.appendChild(el);
      })
    });
}
  </script>
</body>
```

The `fetchPage()` function just fetches the data from the URL that must be supplied as a parameter and checks if there is a next page. If there is, it recursively calls itself again with the new URL.

We then map over the JSON data from the API and create a new `<li>` node for every repository under this organization, and append it to the list.

Let's start the app!

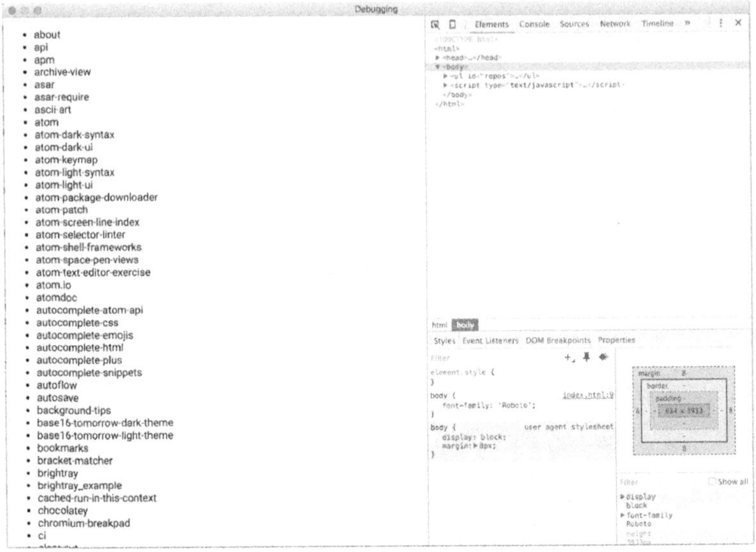

This already looks great and does exactly what we want: shows all of the Github repositories of the atom organization.

Let's have a look at the "Network" tab and check out how many requests were made:

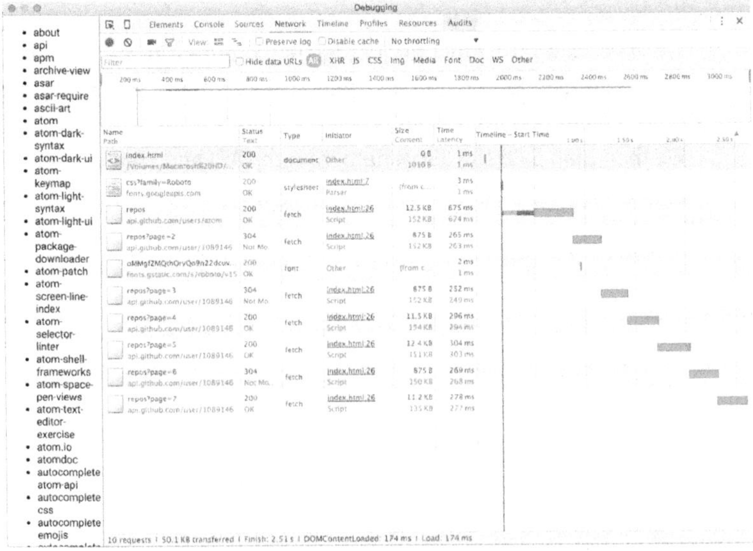

Apparently we needed to do 7 calls to get through all of the pages! We do see the requests that were made for the included Google font. It totals at a load time of 174ms.

As you can see, the requests were made sequentially, because you had to wait for a request to finish before getting the new URL to fetch.

Main process

Now you've seen that debugging the renderer processes is really easy with the Chrome DevTools, because they are just websites. The main process runs in a Node runtime and it's significantly harder to debug.

While `console.log()` statements are often very helpful, they are often just not enough. The "debugging the main process" part is expected to get easier, but for now we have to follow a lot of steps. Let's take the example from before.

node-gyp prerequisites

`node-gyp` is a command-line tool for compiling native add-on modules for Node. You need a special version of this to install all of the **required prerequisites** for it.

On Mac OS X this is `python` 2.7, which is already installed, and `Xcode`.

node-inspector

Node inspector is a debugger interface for Node applications that uses the Blink (Chrome) Developer Tools. The project itself is sponsored by **StrongLoop**.

It is a good tool to debug Node applications with, and it's really easy to use. Debugging a Node application can be done as follows:

```
node-debug app.js
```

You then have access to the Chrome DevTools JavaScript debugger and can inspect variables and step through your code.

For Electron it's not that easy, though.

You need to install it to your working directory: `npm install node-inspector`

Patched version of node-pre-gyp

node-pre-gyp makes it easy to publish and install Node C++ add-ons from binaries, and stands somewhere in between npm and node-gyp.

You need a specially patched version of it:

```
npm install git+https://git@github.com/enlight/node-pre-
gyp.git#detect-electron-runtime-in-find
```

Recompiling the node-inspector v8 modules for Electron

You need to recompile the `node-inspector` native modules to actually work with Electron. For that, you first need to know the exact version of Electron that you're running. Please do the following to find out:

`node_modules/.bin/electron -v`

We are running `v0.36.9`, but you will probably have a newer version of it already.

We need to patch the `v8-debug` and `v8-profiler` modules, so we need to know where they've been installed. If you're running `npm@2.x`, they are probably under `node_modules/node-inspector/node_modules/`. But, if you're already running `npm@3.x`, they are directly in your `node_modules/` folder. Please do check where they are and use the correct path in the following instructions.

Let's recompile the modules:

```
node_modules/.bin/node-pre-gyp --target=0.36.9 --
runtime=electron --fallback-to-build --directory
node_modules/v8-debug/ --dist-url=https://atom.io/download/
atom-shell reinstall
node_modules/.bin/node-pre-gyp --target=0.36.9 --
runtime=electron --fallback-to-build --directory
node_modules/v8-profiler/ --dist-url=https://atom.io/
download/atom-shell reinst
```

Enable debug mode in Electron

To start your application in debug mode, instead of just running `electron .`, do `electron --debug=5858 .` or `electron --debug-brk=5858` to break on the first line.

Start the node-inspector server

Now you need to start the node-inspector server to connect to the running process:

```
ELECTRON_RUN_AS_NODE=true node_modules/.bin/electron
node_modules/node-inspector/bin/inspector.js
```

Load the debugger UI

Now we're ready for debugging. Open the following URL in your Chrome browser: **http://127.0.0.1:8080/debug?ws=127.0.0.1:8080&port=5858**.

If you've chosen to run Electron with the `debug-brk` flag, you may need to click on "Pause" first in the debugger to see the entry line.

You now have access to the same debugger that you used for the renderer process, but now you can debug the main process.

If you want to create a breakpoint from the code, just add `debugger;` and the JavaScript debugger will stop on that line for you so that you can step through the application from this breakpoint on.

Summary

As you've learned, debugging is very important and can give you additional insights into your application and the way it behaves. With Chrome's DevTools, debugging the renderer processes is easy and works exactly the same as it does for a webpage. You can even interactively run code in the "Console" tab or inspect all the scripts you've loaded in the "Resources" tab.

When it comes to debugging the main process, some additional effort is required. It is, however, interesting to be able to go through the process step-by-step and inspect all initialized variables. And after you've set that up the first time, it's really easy!

9 Using Native Node Modules

Node and npm make it easy to develop modules that everybody can use. And they also make it easy to get those with npm. For a standard Node project you have dozens of additional modules you can use.

Usually, those modules enhance the functionality that Node provides in a certain way. For instance, you can connect to your favorite API or do some calculations. They are mostly written in pure JavaScript or some other language that compiles to JavaScript, such as CoffeeScript or Typescript.

There are, however, some use cases where JavaScript is just not enough. Think for example about a database that needs to perform at a high level, or a library that needs to have access to some very specific hardware ports. Those modules are usually written in a lower-level language like C/C++ or Rust.

Luckily, Node supports modules that are written in C/C++. They are called Addons, and they dynamically link shared objects that can be loaded into Node using the standard `require()` function. They are primarily used to provide an interface between JavaScript running in Node and C/C++ libraries. Popular examples of Node Addons are: **`mysql-libmysqlclient`**, which provides binary MySQL bindings for Node, **`leveldown`**, a low-level Node binding to **LevelDB** or **`libxmljs`**, a parser for XML files.

In this chapter we'll write a small native module, and then try to use it (and another, more popular one) inside an Electron application.

Writing a Native Addon

Writing an Addon for Node is rather complicated, and in addition to knowing C/C++, it involves knowing a lot about v8 (the JavaScript implementation that Node uses that is written by Google for it's Chrome browser) and libuv.

Node is well known for its unique asynchronous style and possibility to do non-blocking IO operations using streams and callback functions. What may seem complicated to new users of the language is very popular with more experienced Node developers. All of that asynchronism is being achieved through libuv. libuv is a C library that implements the event-loop and all of the asynchronous behaviors of the platform. It also abstracts file system and network calls across all major desktop platforms.

So you need to know how libuv works and how you can use various parts of it and you also need to know about internal Node C/C++ APIs that you can use if you want to develop an Addon for Node. So you can see, it's really complex. Let us build one!

We'll build a small calculator Addon for Node, which we can use from our JavaScript code. It probably won't be any faster than a simple JavaScript program, but this is to show you how it can be done.

Let's create a new project `native-addons` and do a `npm init`. This is to build a small calculator, so please create a new file called `calculator.cc`.

This is the code for it:

```
#include <node.h>

namespace calculator {

  using v8::FunctionCallbackInfo;
  using v8::Isolate;
  using v8::Local;
  using v8::Object;
  using v8::String;
  using v8::Number;
  using v8::Value;

  void Method(const FunctionCallbackInfo<Value>& args) {
    Isolate* isolate = args.GetIsolate();

    double value = args[0]->NumberValue() + args[1]-
>NumberValue();
    Local<Number> num = Number::New(isolate, value);

    args.GetReturnValue().Set(num);
  }
```

```
  void init(Local<Object> exports) {
    NODE_SET_METHOD(exports, "add", Method);
  }

  NODE_MODULE(addon, init)
}
```

This may look a bit terrifying (or at least not familiar), but it's just C++ code. The logic of the module here is implemented in the `Method`. Basically, you get the two arguments and add them, setting the result as the return value for the function. For the sake of simplicity we do no checks. If a user enters less than two numbers, or one of the arguments is a string, the program will fail.

We won't take too deep of a look at the C/C++ code, but if it interests you, you can read more about it on the **official Addons documentation**.

We can't access the raw C++ code written from the Node program, because it must first be compiled. For that you need a file called `bindings.gyp` that looks like this:

```
{
  "targets": [
    {
      "target_name": "addon",
      "sources": [ "calculator.cc" ]
    }
  ]
}
```

This file is used by `node-gyp`, a tool that compiles native Node Addons. `node-gyp` comes pre-bundled with Node, and is being used when you download a native Addon via npm. However, if you want to use it directly (and we want to use it directly for our sample), you have to install it from npm first: `npm install -g node-gyp`.

You need to run `node-gyp configure` in your project's directory, which will create all of the needed project build files for the current platform in the `build/` directory.

On OS X the generated `build/` folder looks like this:

```
build
├── Makefile
├── addon.target.mk
├── binding.Makefile
├── config.gypi
└── gyp-mac-tool
```

Now you can build the Addon by running `node-gyp build`, which will generate the compiled `addon.node` file that is put in the `build/Release/` directory.

Let's create a Node application `main.js` and use the super calculator Addon:

```
const addon = require('./build/Release/addon');

console.log(addon.add(1, 99));
```

If you run this application, you can see that the calculation it did is correct: 1 + 99 is indeed 100. Great job!

Using Native Addons

Now let's create an Electron application where you use a Node native Addon that actually does something usable. LevelDB is a light-weight key/value data store with bindings to many platforms that was developed by Google and is used inside Chrome and other products.

There is a Node Addon called `leveldown` that serves as a binding to a LevelDB instance and there's a higher abstraction called `levelup`. LevelUP exposes the features of LevelDB in a "Node-friendly way" using Node streams.

Because levelUP became so popular, people started building other backends for it. You can easily replace your LevelDB data store with a relational MySQL database or just use a in-memory replacement, which is really useful for writing unit tests.

There's also a whole lot modules available that build on top of LevelDB and provide additional functionality. There is a list on **LevelUPs Wiki**.

Our next small project is going to be a Note-taking application that actually persists the data using LevelDB. For that we'll create a new folder, but you can copy the `package.json` and `main.js` files from the previous example. We need to reinstall `electron-prebuilt` and introduce two new modules: `levelup` and `leveldown`.

```
npm install --save electron-prebuilt levelup leveldown
```

In the `index.html` file we will create a LevelDB instance using `levelup`:

```
<!doctype html>
<html>
<head>
  <meta charset="utf-8">
  <title>Native Addons</title>
</head>
<body>
  <script type="text/javascript">

const levelup = require('levelup');
const db = levelup('./db');

  </script>
</body>
</html>
```

If you run this example you'll see in the DeveloperTools console that there was an error accessing the `leveldown` module that `levelup` automatically requires.

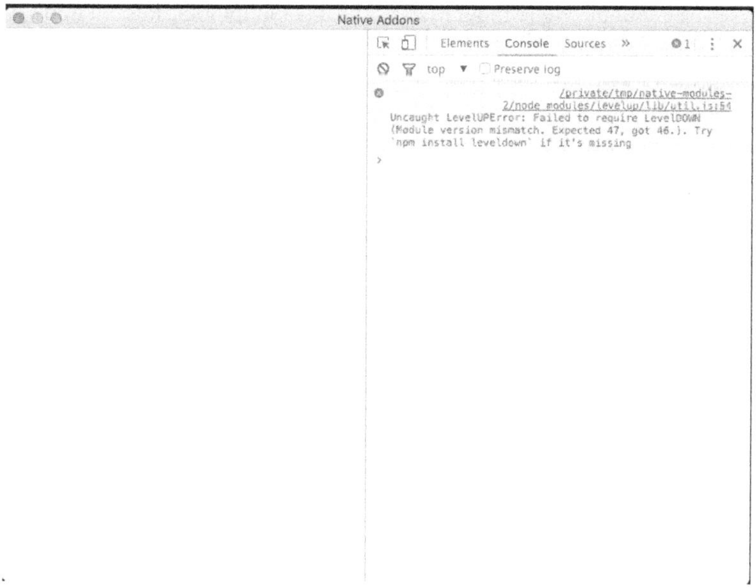

Now, the problem here is the way Native Addons get built. If you install `leveldown` from the npm registry, npm automatically builds the module against the locally installed Node version, which is great for every Node project. Electron ships it's own Node version, and unless the locally installed version and the Electron version are the same, the module won't work.

So, what you have to do is rebuild the `leveldown` module against the proper Node version that we're using inside Electron.

This can be done as follows:

```
cd node_modules/leveldown
node-gyp rebuild --target=0.37.2 --arch=x86 --dist-
url=https://atom.io/download/atom-shell
```

(Please replace `0.37.2` with your Electron version.)

Now if you start the application again, there is no more error. Every Native Addon module you want to use inside your application needs to be rebuilt against the right Electron version.

There is a project called **`electron-rebuild`** that strives to make this process easier. It unfortunately doesn't work all of the time, and it did not work for `leveldown`.

The database is ready, so let's start building the app!

First of all, we're moving all of the JavaScript logic into an `app.js` file to ensure the readability of our code. In the `index.html` file include the `app.js` file:

```
<script type="text/javascript" src="app.js"></script>
```

This app will let you create TODOs, so you create a simple text input, a button, and a (empty) list to be able to do so:

```
<h1>Electron Todo</h1>
<input type="text" id="text-input"><button id="add-todo">Add
Todo</button>
<ul id="list-of-todos"></ul>
```

That's it for the HTML code. Let's implement the logic now in the `app.js` file.

You're gonna need an additional module **`uuid`** to generate unique IDs for the TODOs, so please install that too: `npm install uuid --save`

```
const levelup = require('levelup');
const uuid = require('uuid');

const db = levelup('./db', { valueEncoding: 'json' });

const listOfTodos = document.getElementById('list-of-todos');
```

```
const textInput = document.getElementById('text-input');
const addTodoButton = document.getElementById('add-todo');
```

This is a basic setup. The `valueEncoding` parameter specifies what encoding LevelDB should use for the values. This means that you can store JavaScript objects in them and they get encoded in the JSON format.

The next thing to do is listen to clicks on the button and create a new TODO with the text the user has entered:

```
addTodoButton.addEventListener('click', () => {
  var text = textInput.value;
  if (!text) return;

  var id = uuid();
  var todo = {
    text: text,
    done: false
  };
  db.put(id, todo, (err) => {
    if (err) console.error(err);

    textInput.value = ''; // reset input field
    displayTodo(id, todo); // not yet implemented
  });
});
```

Now, when a user enters a text and hits the button, a new TODO is being stored in the database. Now, you need to implement the logic for `displayTodo()`:

```
function displayTodo (id, todo) {
  var checkbox = document.createElement('input');
  checkbox.type = 'checkbox';
  checkbox.onclick = toggleTodoDone.bind(this, id); // not
yet implemented
  checkbox.checked = (todo.done ? true : false);

  var textSpan = document.createElement('span');
  textSpan.textContent = todo.text;

  var li = document.createElement('li');
  li.appendChild(checkbox);
  li.appendChild(textSpan);
```

```
    listOfTodos.appendChild(li);
  }
```

Create a `<li>`-element and append a checkbox that has the value of `todo.done` and a simple `<span>`-element for the text of the TODO.

When you run this, you can already add TODOs that are going to be persisted in the database.

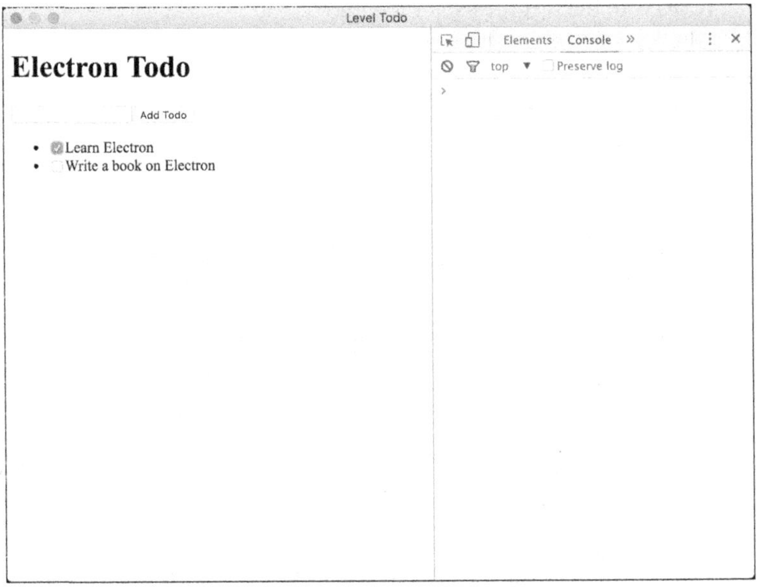

While we do persist all of the TODOs in the database, we don't yet persist their `done` state. Let's implement the `toggleTodoDone` function that we've already set as our `onclick` listener:

```
function toggleTodoDone (id) {
  db.get(id, (err, todo) => {
    if (err) console.error(err);

    todo.done = !todo.done;
    db.put(id, todo, (err) => {
      if (err) console.error(err);
    });
  });
}
```

This is pretty straight-forward. First, fetch the TODO from the database by its ID, and then toggle the **done** attribute, saving it again to the database.

The only thing that's missing now is that we need to display the TODOs that were persisted before. A user creates a TODO, quits the app, opens the app again, and the TODO is still there.

Let's add the following lines right after the initialization of the database:

```
db.createReadStream().on('data', (data) => {
  displayTodo(data.key, data.value);
});
```

Use LevelDB's streaming functionality to create a ReadStream on the database. For each record, apply the `displayTodo()` function.

If you close the app and open it again, you can see the exact same TODOs with their correct **done** state.

While using Node Native Addons is not trivial (especially if the locally installed Node version isn't the same as the one Electron uses), they help enhance the application in a very powerful way.

Summary

Here we've written a small Native Addon that we then used inside a Node application.

You probably won't write that many Native Addons yourself, but there's a high chance that if you're building a bigger Electron application, you'll want to use a specific Native Addon like we used LevelDB in our latest experiment.

Electron Versus the Web 10

It's clear by now how powerful Electron is. It doesn't take much effort to create a complex desktop application using Electron, you get to leverage your existing skills with Web technologies, and a user can easily have no idea your app isn't native. Win, win, win. The use of Web technologies is really interesting. Does this afford you anything you couldn't do in a native desktop app? Does it limit you in any way? This is what we'll explore in this chapter.

Sure, there are advantages to going native. Native APIs make it easy to do certain things, some of which are completely impossible to achieve on the Web. Thankfully, you can use native modules or binaries if you really need to. One example we'll take a look at is detecting when the user is "away from keyboard."

On the other side, it's amazing what can be achieved in a Web browser these days. Thanks to the fact that we're shipping a browser to users as part of our app, we can leverage the latest and greatest tools currently available to Web developers. As you'll see, these include cutting-edge HTML5 APIs, CSS3 layout modules, and more. We'll also take a look at a few of the issues that arise from using Web technologies with `file://` URLs.

Our app lives in a sweet spot in which the Web and the desktop overlap. You won't need to use native APIs most of the time, though. Web technologies often win. This will be illustrated later when we figure out how to determine if the user has a solid network connection at any given time.

Going even further, what's stopping us from reusing the one code base for both the Web and the desktop? Well, a little thing or two, but it is completely possible. We'll also discuss this some more throughout this chapter.

Exploiting browser lock-in

The beautiful thing about Electron is that you know that 100% of your users are using a recent version of Chromium. A whole host of bleeding edge features are now accessible, which you wouldn't usually use if you were making a typical Web app due to spotty browser support. You have no more worrying about a degraded experience for a portion of your users, adding fallbacks and polyfills. Either 100% of your users support something, or none of them do. This is liberating for any Web developer. Let's take a quick look at some of these shiny new tools in our toolbox.

Battery status

Yes, there's an API for all battery related statistics thanks to HTML5. This is a pretty cool (promise-based) API to use in your desktop app. In the following example, we use one of the many events to keep track of the current battery level:

```
navigator.getBattery().then((battery) => {
  battery.addEventListener('levelchange', () => {
    console.log("Battery level: " + battery.level * 100 +
"%");
  });
});
```

WebSockets

How would you like real-time data transfer from and to the server? "WebSocket" is a protocol providing full-duplex communication channels over a single TCP connection. With the HTML5 WebSockets API, you can send messages to a server and receive event-driven responses without having to poll the server for a reply.

```
var ws = new WebSocket("ws://localhost:9998");

ws.onopen = () => {
   // We're connected
   ws.send("Message to send");
};

ws.onmessage = (event) => {
   console.log(event.data);
};
```

```
ws.onclose = () => {
   // WebSocket connection is closed
};
```

You may be aware of WebSocket libraries like Socket.IO or similar. These are really good and rightly popular, because they have a lot of fallbacks (like long-polling, etc.) if WebSockets aren't supported. Since we know they'll be supported in Electron, the overhead of a wrapper library is unnecessary. This is great for performance, because pure WebSockets are really fast.

Device orientation

There are a few handy events for tracking when the current device's orientation changes or even when it moves.

Be aware that the specification for this is still subject to change.

```
window.addEventListener("deviceorientation", (event) => {
  var alpha = event.alpha; // motion in degrees around z-axis
  var beta = event.beta; // same but around x-axis
  var gamma = event.gamma; // same but around y-axis

  // do something cool here
}, true);

window.addEventListener("devicemotion", (event) => {
    console.log(event.acceleration,
event.accelerationIncludingGravity, event.rotatationRate);
}, true);
```

Speech

The Web Speech API allows you to do some voice recognition and speech synthesis, such as generating speech from text. Here is a simple one-liner:

```
window.speechSynthesis.speak(new
SpeechSynthesisUtterance('Hello World'));
```

This is just the tip of the iceberg.

Audio

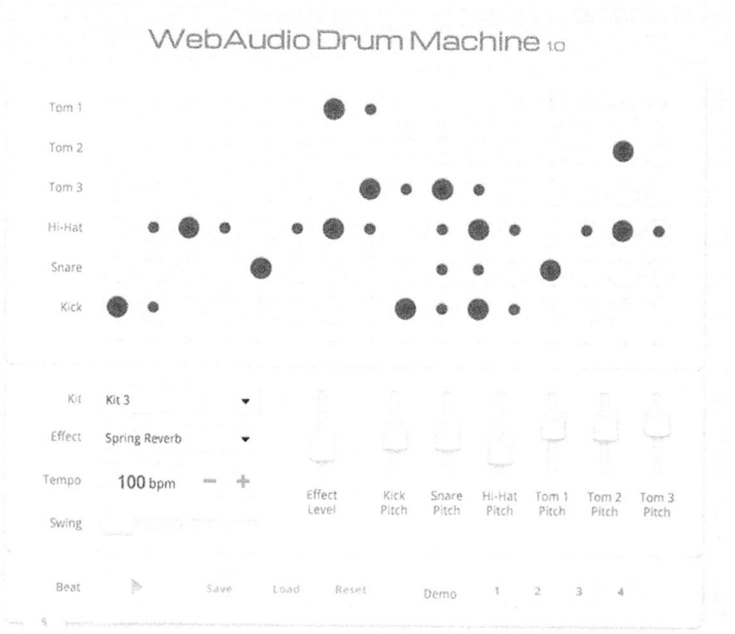

The Web Audio API provides a lot of power and flexibility when it comes to controlling audio on the Web. You can configure audio sources, add all sorts of crazy effects and visualizations, and a lot more. The sky is the limit.

```
var context = new AudioContext();
var oscillator = context.createOscillator();

oscillator.connect(context.destination);
oscillator.start(context.currentTime);
oscillator.stop(context.currentTime + 1);
```

MIDI

There's a Web MIDI (Musical Instrument Digital Interface) API as well.

```
navigator.requestMIDIAccess().then((midi) => {
  // boom boom boom
});
```

With this, you can send input from physical musical instruments like keyboards or MIDI controllers, and even send instructions to any connected MIDI output. Just imagine what you can do with the Web Audio API and a <canvas> element.

Web components

```
<template id="nameTemplate">
<style>
  ...
</style>
<div class="wrapper">
  <div class="intro">
    Hi, I'm
  </div>
  <div class="name">
    <content></content>
  </div>
</div>
</template>
```

Web Components consists of these four technologies (although each can be used separately):

- Custom Elements
- HTML Templates
- Shadow DOM
- HTML Imports

Web components will pave the way for better encasuplated and reusable widgets.

Service worker

Service workers lie between your Web applications, and the browser and network (if there is any), facilitating "offline-first" apps via caching, network request mocking, push notifications and background syncronization of data. Watch this space.

```
self.addEventListener('fetch', (event) => {
  console.log('Handling fetch event for', event.request.url);

  event.respondWith(
    //...
```

```
  );
});
```

Visuals

Create complex graphics with WebGL, peer-to-peer video calls with WebRTC or ORTC, and more.

```
// Initialize the GL context
var gl = initWebGL(document.getElementById('canvas'));

if (gl) {
  // Set clear color to black, fully opaque
  gl.clearColor(0.0, 0.0, 0.0, 1.0);
  // Clear the color as well as the depth buffer.
  gl.clear(gl.COLOR_BUFFER_BIT | gl.DEPTH_BUFFER_BIT);
}
```

CSS3 layout modules

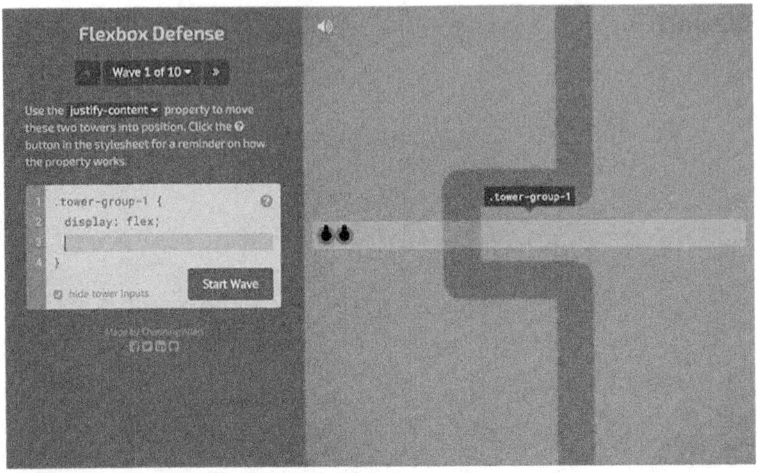

The CSS3 flexible box module is the future of layout. Not only does it simplify a lot of previously tricky problems, but it's also very efficient. With flexbox, it's easy to lay out, align, and distribute space among items in a container, without having to set heights or widths.

```
.wrapper {
  display: flex;
  flex-direction: column-reverse;
  align-items: flex-end;
}

.item {
  flex: 1;
}

.item--wide {
 flex: 3;
}
```

CSS3 also affords Electron users the ability to create multi-column layouts, regions, exclusions, and grids.

Barebones DOM manipulation

Inspired by great libraries, you can now painlessly grab elements, manipluate them, quickly toggle classes without hassle, and more, all natively. We've come a long way.

```
document.querySelector('.a > .b').classList.add('c');
```

localStorage

Ok, localStorage has been around awhile, but yes, it available to use in Electron, and it's so convenient.

```
localStorage.clear(); // totally empty localStorage
localStorage.setItem('type', 'something');

// ...

var type = localStorage.getItem('type');

if(type && type === 'something'){
  // do something

  localStorage.removeItem('type');
}
```

localStorage allows you to securely store key/value pairs (exclusive to the current user) very easily, without the need for cookies. This can come in handy for remembering the user's settings for your app.

Note that you can only store simple values. If you want to store objects then you'll need a wrapper library like store, which gives you the ability while abstracting the messiness of achieving it away from you.

Just like Web browsers, the data is stored on disk. Unlike Web browsers, it's not stored within or near your app, but in C:\Users\<user-name>\AppData\Local\<app-name>\ or ~/Library/Application Data/<app-name>/ for example. This means that if the user was to delete your app and re-install it, there's a good chance your localStorage data will still be there. Please take that into account.

Reminder: never reference these paths directly; use app.getPath.

Detecting connectivity

The Electron documentation itself contains examples leveraging HTML5 APIs, including **one article** showing how to detect if the user has a network connection or not. This can be done in a renderer process like so:

```
<script>
  var alertOnlineStatus = (event) => {
    window.alert(navigator.onLine ? 'online' : 'offline');
  };

  window.addEventListener('online',  alertOnlineStatus);
  window.addEventListener('offline',  alertOnlineStatus);

  alertOnlineStatus();
</script>
```

You can use the `navigator.onLine` property to check the status at any given time, and there are also `online` and `offline` events fired by the `window` when it changes.

Note: the `event` argument passed to either callback will contain a `type` property containing either `online` or `offline`.

You should use publish IPC events if you want to use this in your main process.

This API is unreliable though. As the **specification** itself says:

```
window.navigator.onLine
```

This returns `false` if the user agent is definitely offline (disconnected from the network). It returns `true` if the user agent might be online.

This results in false positives when you are connected to *a* network, but not the Internet. For instance, false positives occur when your connection is flaky, when you've just reconnected, or if you have a virtual LAN adapter (this happens if you use VirtualBox or similar).

Service worker, which we touched on earlier, is often used to create "offline-first" apps. With Electron, you kind of get that for free. Since all you're files are local files, your app will load whether you have a connection or not. Of course, more can be achieved with a service worker, like caching remote requests, etc. Theoretically though, you can also cache data to disk instead, but ultimately, service workers are a big step forward for the Web and will unlock many doors.

Is there anyone out there?

So how can you reliable check if you have a live connection? You need to actually try to request or ping something, but what? Something that definitely can't be down. That makes sense, right? That would be one of the thirteen "root servers". From **Wikipedia**:

A root name server is a name server for the root zone of the Domain Name System of the Internet. It directly answers requests for records in the root zone and answers other requests by returning a list of the authoritative name servers for the appropriate top-level domain (TLD). The root name servers are a critical part of the Internet infrastructure because they are the first step in translating (resolving) human readable host names into IP addresses that are used in communication between Internet hosts.

If the server responds, you know you're online. This is a simplistic overview of how the lovely **`is-online`** module works. Once you grab it from npm, it can be used in place of `navigator.onLine` like this:

```
const isOnline = require('is-online');

isOnline((err, online) => {
  console.log(online); // true
});
```

This is the entire API. Yes, that means there are no `online` or `offline` events unfortunately, but you could call this continuously, like when a request fails.

`navigator.onLine` can result in false positives, but never false negatives. If it says you're offline, you definitely don't have a connection. Thanks to that, it can save trying to ping somewhere if you use it in conjunction with `is-online`;

```
const isOnline = require('is-online');

if(navigator.onLine){
    isOnline((err, online) => {
        // we're online if online is true, offline if false
    });
}
else {
  // we're offline
}
```

Watch out for protocol-less URLs

```
Failed to load resource: net::ERR_FILE_NOT_FOUND
```

You might come across that error one day. You are, or a dependency of yours (which is usually only used by typical Web developers) is using a **protocol-relative URL**; for example:

```
fetch('//s3.amazonaws.com/something/blah').then(() => {
    //...
});
```

If that code was in a script used by a page accessed over HTTPS, HTTPS will be used as the protocol when requesting this URL, or HTTP if the page was accessed over HTTP. But the protocol in this case is neither HTTP nor HTTPs; our `index.html` is a local file and accessed as such. In this case, this URL would be expanded to `file:///s3.amazonaws.com...`. So, if you want your Web app to work on the desktop, avoid protocol-relative URLs. To fix this line, you need to have something like the following:

```
var scheme = window.location.protocol === 'file:' ?
'https:' : window.location.protocol;
fetch(scheme + '//s3.amazonaws.com/something/blah').then(()
=> {
    //...
});
```

These days, developers can't possibly think of every possible use case and environment their code could be used for, so keep an eye out. Be nice and submit a pull-request whenever possible.

Spell checking

Spelling isn't always easy, especially when you don't know you've mispelled something. This is more likely when using a long word you rarely use, when you're new to a language, or if you have dyslexia. If your app takes user input, it must have spell checking functionality.

Spell checking comes for free on the Web because it's built into browsers and can be extended further with extensions (P.S. check out **Helper Bird** if you're dyslexic). Typically, a mispelled word is underlined by a red squiggly line and suggested corrections can be found in the context menu.

What about Electron apps? Well, that's where the `webFrame` module comes in;

```
const webFrame = require('electron').webFrame;
const spellChecker = require('spellchecker');

webFrame.setSpellCheckProvider('en-US', true, {
  spellCheck: (text) => !spellChecker.isMisspelled(text)
});
```

`webFrame.setSpellCheckProvider` accepts a language (or locale), a `autoCorrectWord` Boolean, which you should set to `true`, and a `provider`. The `provider` must be an object that has a `spellCheck` method, which will be called with a single string parameter and must return a Boolean indicating if the text is spelled correctly or not. The rest is up to you. You must decide if the word is misspelled. Thankfully, there are a handful of spell checking modules on npm, including `spellchecker` (created by the Atom team).

The example above corrects spelling based on American English, which won't suit everyone. You could ask users for their preferred language and pass it to `setSpellCheckProvider`, but the ideal thing to do would be to automatically detect it.

```
const electron = require('electron');
const app = electron.app;
const webFrame = electron.webFrame;
const spellChecker = require('spellchecker');

app.on('ready', () => {
  webFrame.setSpellCheckProvider(app.getLocale(), true, {
    spellCheck: (text) => !spellChecker.isMisspelled(text))
  });
});
```

As you can see, you can grab the system locale using `app.getLocale`. You need to wait until the app's `ready` callback is fired, because operating systems tend not to provide information like this until the app is up and running fully.

webFrame

What is `webFrame` anyway? It's an Electron module that allows you to do some things you're accustomed to on the Web, including customizing how a Web page is rendered. It can only be used in a renderer process, therefore only affecting the current window.

It has a lot of different uses. You can pass a string containing JavaScript to `webFrame.executeJavaScript` to run it in the page. It allows you to tweak some URL scheme stuff, as well as providing zoom-related methods, including `getZoomFactor`, `setZoomLevel`, and `getZoomLevelLimits`.

Shortcuts

Since Electron has the `globalShorcut` API, you may be tempted to use that for all shortcuts. I mean, even use it for shortcuts which are fired when the app is focused. If you want those to work in the Web, you'll have to rewrite the registrations to use a library like **Mousetrap** or similar. Besides, it is a bit careless anyway. Even if you were to check if the app is focused in your callback(s), binding all your keyboard shortcuts with `globalShortcut` could block other apps' shortcuts from working when your app is no longer focused.

Be careful what you wish for

Before you go too crazy using all of bleeding-edge HTML5 APIs at your disposal in Electron, there's one thing you should consider. If you ever plan to reuse your app code for Web as well as the desktop (which is an easily achieved and attractive option), you may need to add polyfills, fallbacks, or even remove something cool.

Won't I have bigger problems than that?

Oh, well yeah. Of course you'll need to not call any Node or Electron code while your app is running in the Web. You can do this by checking if `process.versions.electron` exists.

```
const doesElectronExist = typeof process === 'object' &&
typeof process.versions === 'object' && typeof
process.versions.electron === 'string';

if(doesElectronExist){
  const electron = require('electron');
  //...
}
```

Oh and you know the way you've `required` browser scripts from other scripts? Yeah, that'll break too. So you would have to use **Browserify**, **Webpack**, or similar module bundlers, to traverse all of the `requires` and bundle all your scripts up into something compatible.

Basically, you would run a command like `browserify app.js -o bundle.js` (or use the bundler API programmatically in a script) and in return it'll spit out a single script to be consumed by your Web app. This script would contain a browser implementation of the `require()` function and all of the required modules. So just one `<script>` is needed, no matter how many `requires` you have.

It's probably not a big deal, but a downside to this is that you can end up with a little bit of redundant code in the browser. So, if you actually have a different build process (or command, etc.) for making your Web build, then you can set `doesElectronExist` at build-time, passing it to Browserify (or similar). If you're using Browserify in particular, check out the **`envify`** module (or "transform" as its known in Browserify-land), which allows you to set environment variables.

```
if(process.env.doesElectronExist){
  const platform = require('./platform.js');
  // ...
}
```

If you were to pass a `doesElectronExist` variable to `envify`, any reference to `process.env.doesElectronExist` in your code would be replaced with its actual value in the resultant JavaScript file, such as `if(process.env.doesElectronExist){` would become `if(false){`.

Then when Browserify is doing its static analysis, parsing and traversing `requires`, this becomes very useful. Knowing it shouldn't go beyond an `if(false){` guard, Browserify would ignore any `requires` inside. It wouldn't bundle in our platform detection module (`platform.js`) for the Web build, for example. By dropping the dead weight, we end up with just the right code for the browser. The least amount of bytes we need to download in the browser, the better.

```
app.on('ready', () => {
 mainWindow = new BrowserWindow({
  width: 800,
  height: 600,
  webPreferences: {
   nodeIntegration: false
  }
 });
 mainWindow.loadURL('file://' + __dirname + '/index.html');
})
```

You learned previously of the specific options the `BrowserWindow` class contructor accepts. One of those, the `nodeIntegration` attribute, totally changes how you can use Electron. If set to `false`, you can turn off Node.js for the new window. However, if you do choose to not make use of the Node.js integration, e.g. for security reasons, you won't have access to the `require` function. So this is another use case in which module bundlers would be useful.

Back to the future

We have more bad news. `const` (and its ES2015/ES6 friends) aren't exactly well-supported, yet. The oldest browser that supports `const` is Internet Explorer 11. You can either remove the usage completely or else use something to polyfill (or rather transpile) it, like Babel, Closure Compiler, or Rollup.

Local before CDN

If you're trying to make the best Web app you can make, you'll end eventually using a CDN (Content Delivery Network) for your assets. Your assets could be cached in mutiple “edge locations” or servers around the world closer to users, to drastically reduce latency and reducing improve load time for your Web app. This is great, but stick with `file://` for your assets within your desktop app, because loading local files is pretty much instantaneous.

There’s no limit on concurrent requests to `file://` URLs. Usually Chrome, for example, limits the number of requests it allows to be ongoing to the one domain. For the Web, using a CDN is often used to get around that by doing domain-sharding (using more domains).

Note: that approach will be redudant once HTTP 2.0 is commonly used.

Away from keyboard

One thing that’s impossible to do reliably in Web browsers is detect when the user is “away from keyboard”. In other words, when the user hasn’t interacted (via their mouse, keyboard, touchpad, or any other peripheral) in awhile and is likely away from their machine.

You can write a small bit of JavaScript that listens for a few different events (key presses, mouse movements), but this would only catch interactions in the browser tab your code is running in. A user could playing an intense game of Tetris in another tab, but as far as your code is concerns, they’re idle.

It is possible to create your own browser app or extension to oversee all of the tabs, but this is not a real solution. In fact, it isn’t even *a* solution at all but multiple solutions, or an exclusive solution per browser. That just doesn’t feel right. A given browser might even support the APIs required or allow communication between your extension and your tabs. Even if you did put in all of this effort and managed to convince users to install the extension (good luck!), then this would only detect when the user interacts with their browser. A developer buried in their editor looks like they’re never at their computer.

This is why something like Electron is great. It brings web and native APIs together, allowing you to do things you couldn’t do before. We built a nice little module at Teamwork.com that we can use here. It’s called **`afk`** and it’s on npm. In the following example, we log to the console whenever the user is away for ten seconds:

```
const afk = require('afk');
const seconds = 10;
```

```
var listenerId = afk.addListener(seconds, (event) => {
    console.log(event);
});

// To stop listening:
// afk.removeListener(listenerId);
```

The callback passed to `afk.addListener` is also called when the user interacts again for the first time after being idle for the given time. The `event` argument contains the following properties:

- `id`: the listener ID.
- `status`: either `away` or `back`.
- `seconds`: the number of seconds passed to `addListener`.

That's it. Underneath, `afk` uses native platform-specific APIs or commands to calculate the system-wide idle time.

Automated testing

Let's not get into too much detail here (it's a massive separate topic), but suffice it to say that you can test your desktop app like you would a web app with Mocha, Chai, Nightwatch and more. You might have to jump through some hoops to get Selenium WebDriver style integration tests running *inside* your application, but you don't need to. Since your app is just HTML, CSS, and JavaScript, you can just run your tests on those files outside your app instead.

Summary

As you can see, you can do some truly impressive things on the desktop with HTML5 and web technologies, from checking the device's battery or network connection, to drawing advanced graphics or tapping into physical instruments, and more. Although, you might run into issues when working with `file://` URLs or, maybe more accurately, module developers who are unaware of the desktop as a potential environment for their code.

Yet, there is a time and a place for native code, as you saw with `afk`. It's great to have access to all the power of Web technologies, Node.js, and native APIs, all at once. It would be pretty selfish to keep it to ourselves, so let's take a thorough look at distributing our app to end users in the next chapter.

Distributing Your App 11

So, you want to create real distributable apps from your code? Great. To be a true desktop app, it should be a self-contained `.exe`, `.app`, or similar. Let's take a thorough look at the entire process. There may be a few more concerns here than you might anticipate. We'll cover how to package up your app, handle branding, create installers, and so on. What you might not have expected, though, is that you have to deal with path length and permissions problems, aggresive anti-virus software, weight concerns, and code signing (your app *and* your dependencies). We also touch on concealing your code from preying eyes and automating the distribution process.

Are you scared yet? Shipping your app does indeed bring a few extra concerns to the table, but don't be intimated, because the required code and effort won't be overwhelming. We will cover some of the pitfalls, for your own sake, in this chapter. Hopefully you'll learn from the mistakes we've made. Don't worry though, we won't throw you in the deep end. Let's examine how to manually create executables to begin with.

First, create a new directory called `dist` at the root of your project. Download a prebuilt binary from **Electron's Releases on GitHub** for the platform you'd like to build for. Ignore the ZIP archives that have `-dsym` or `-symbols` in the name. For Mac, look for `darwin`.

For Windows, grab a `win32-ia32` or `win32-x64` ZIP. The former is the 32-bit build, which will work on any 32-bit or 64-bit Windows, but the latter will only work on 64-bit Windows. So let's stick with `ia32`. Similarly, there's `linux32-ia32` and `linux32-x64` for Linux but be aware that `ia32` will *only* work on 32-bit machines and `x64` only on 64-bit machines. So if you're distributing your app to Linux users, you'll need to build two versions of your app.

Why are there both 32-bit and 64-bit versions for Windows and Mac? Well, basically because Google Chrome released a 64-bit version. Don't worry about it too much. You most likely won't see any difference with your app. Google does claim that the 64-bit version of Chrome is slightly more stable though.

Copy the contents of the ZIP you've downloaded to your new `dist` directory.

Now you need to copy your app code to a specific location (in `dist`), which depends on the platform you're building for. For Windows & Linux, there's an `electron.exe` or `electron` executable. On the same level, there should be a `resources` directory. Delete any existing `app` directory or `.asar` file. Create a directory named `app` inside `resources` and copy your app code there.

For Mac, you need to copy your app code to `Electron.app/Contents/Resources/app/`. Yes, that's inside the app. Mac apps are essentially directories. To open it up, right click `Electron.app` in Finder and click `Show Package Contents`. Again, make sure to delete any existing files in `app` or any `.asar` file in `Resources`. If you see a dialog explaining that the app can't be opened, because it's from an untrusted developer or source, and then right-clicking the app in Finder and clicking "Open" should get around that.

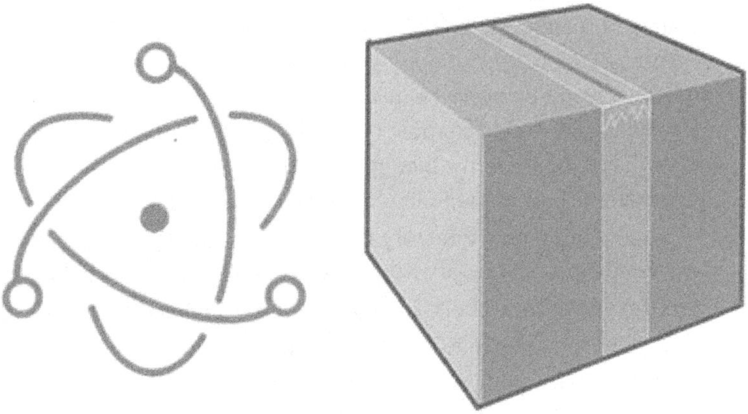

To launch your app, run the Electron executable (`Electron.exe` on Windows, `Electron.app` on Mac, or `electron` on linux). Tada! If you want to distribute this, the `dist` directory is what you should share. It's safe to create a ZIP containing the contents of `dist`.

Rebranding

Since we're reusing Electron's own features here, your app will have the Electron icon and will be named "Electron.exe" on Windows, for example. You can use Atom's `node-rcredit` module, or `rcredit` if you prefer the command-line, to change the icon to your liking. Both are available on npm. You can rename the executables as you wish to, except there's a little bit more to it for your OS X application. You would rename the inner helper applications and would have to edit a few values in a couple of inner `Info.plist` files. Otherwise the app will be corrupted. You could also rebuild Electron from source, using C++ and Objective C++ source code to generate an app with your brand, but that's a lot of hassle. Actually, it's all a bit too much. This should be easier, and it is. We won't go into too much detail here because there's a much better way to handle this, with `electron-packager`, but more about that after we take a look at path length problems and asar archives.

Windows and path length problems

You might have been unfortunate enough to learn that Windows has a 256 character limit on file paths. You could've ran into this problem locally or on end users' machines. A workaround does exist and so do preventive measures we advise you to take. Even if you haven't had this issue yet, it's worth being aware of this if you ever plan to distribute your app to Windows users.

npm

Neither this problem, nor our solution, are exclusive to Node.js, but a lot of the victims of the path length problem are probably running Node.js on Windows. Windows users know that they get left out in the cold often by npm package maintainers, but even **the design of npm itself was a problem on Windows from the get-go**.

npm (< 3.0.0) stores your dependencies (listed in your `package.json`) in a `node_modules` directory. If those dependencies have dependencies of their own, they're stored in their own `node_modules` directory (i.e. `your-project/node_modules/a/node_modules/b/`) and so on recursively. It's nice, but in hindsight it's obviously incompatible with Windows's path length limit.

DELETE DELETE DELETE

Most people have probably only have come across this problem when trying to delete dependencies where then Windows complains that the path is too long.

```
node_modules/a/node_modules/b/node_modules/c/.../
node_modules/h/
node_modules/h/
```

A simple way around this is to take a module halfway down deep into your dependency graph in Windows Explorer and move it somewhere closer to the root to cut the file path down before trying to delete it again. This would have to be repeated for every culprit.

There are also some tools that can help. We've noticed that you can delete really long paths while using **7-Zip** File Manager to browse files.

RUNTIME ERRORS

If you've run into actual bugs caused by this, you can find a module halfway down the dependency graph and add it as a dependency to your project so it will be installed under the top level `node_modules` and not a `node_modules` directory n levels deep. Make sure to install the correct version and test thoroughly.

There are also a few Node modules out there that "flatten" your dependency graph. The downside to these modules is that if there is a conflict (package A depends on version 1.0.0 of package Z and package B depends on version 3.2.1 of package Z) then the latest version of the module (package Z) is used, which can be problematic. So be careful.

CAN'T NPM FIX THIS?

Yes, they, can! This has been fixed as of **npm 3.0.0**.

Your dependencies will now be installed *maximally* flat. Insofar as is possible, all of your dependencies, and their dependencies, and THEIR dependencies will be installed in your project's `node_modules` folder with no nesting. You'll only see modules nested underneath one another when two (or more) modules have conflicting dependencies.

This is really great but some of you may need to stick with an older version of npm (for various reasons) or may have long paths that have nothing to do with npm at all. So let's look at some measures you can take and what happens when you don't.

Manually checking for exceedingly long paths

Up until now, we've had to routinely check for long paths using **Path Length Checker** (on Windows) but a manual check is not good enough as stuff can still slip through the net.

Introducing gulp-path-length

So there's a simple **Gulp** plugin to help with **gulp-path-length**. We created this at Teamwork.com specifically to prevent path length issues from reoccurring. If you don't use Gulp as your task runner, we recommend it. You can use `gulp-path-length` like this in a Gulp task:

```
const gulp = require('gulp');
const pathLength = require('gulp-path-length');

gulp.task('default', () => {
    gulp.src('./example/path/to/directory/**', {read: false})
        .pipe(pathLength());
});
```

If all is well, nothing will happen. If you have a path exceeding 256 characters, the gulp task will stop and an error will reveal the offending path. This is really fast either way because Gulp doesn't need to read the contents of the files. The limit can be changed with a parameter such as `.pipe(pathLength({ maxLength: 50 });`.

This is fine if it's just for you locally, but there are bigger fish to fry.

Distributed long paths

What if there are multiple developers working on your project? What if a developer is using Mac OS X or Linux? There can easily be false positives. It's one thing having issues locally or within a team, it's a different thing to have path length problems in production on end users machines.

Depending on how long the end user's username was, nothing can happen when they tried to launch my app. Either that or they'd see a dummy application. Either way, none of the app code was executed. This means no error reports and there is no way the app can even auto-update once a patch is released.

IS THERE ANYTHING WE CAN DO?

Once the code is shipped, it's too late. Luckily in this case, we had an idea where the files will exist on end user machines thanks to the Windows installer (more about that later). This is where gulp-path-length's `rewrite` option comes in. It can be used like this to simulate path lengths:

```
const gulp = require('gulp');
const pathLength = require('gulp-path-length');

gulp.task('default', () => {
    gulp.src('./example/path/to/directory/**', {read: false})
        .pipe(pathLength({
            rewrite: {
                match: './example/path/to/directory/',
                replacement: 'C:\\Users\\a-long-username-here
\\AppData\\Blah\\Blah\\Blah'
            }
        }));
});
```

So it doesn't matter where you are on your filesystem or what operating system you're using. It will test the length of files in a given directory as if they're in a hypothetical directory on Windows. In the example above, `./example/path/to/directory/` is where your project files are and `C:\\Users\\a-long-username-here\\AppData\\Blah\\Blah\\Blah` is an example place your app might be installed to on Windows users' machines.

You can run this before you ship your code, but we suggest adding this to a compilation build step so you catch it as early as possible. If a Mac developer adds really long paths to the project (like an npm dependency that depends on a chain of **lodash** modules), they'll see right away that this will break stuff for some Windows users. For good measure, I recommend running it in a continuous integration step if that's possible.

Side note: this could also be applied to your development dependencies, since non-Windows users can be made aware if they are to introduce a dependency that would be problematic for colleagues on Windows.

Thankfully, Microsoft seems to want to chip in as well, because Windows 10 makes it a bit harder for you to create file paths that are too long. Hopefully this continues to be tightened with every new version of Windows.

Aha! Asar to the rescue

Fortunately, the character limit does not apply to any files in an asar archive, which we'll cover in due detail next. Nevertheless, it's better to be safe than sorry. It's best to still be aware and have preventive measures in place. Especially as you may decide at any stage to move some of your files outside of the archive. Now, what *is* asar and is this the only reason why you should use it?

Asar

An asar archive is like a tar archive. It's a single file that contains as many files as you choose and Electron can read any one of these files from the archive without unpacking it in its entirety. Not only does it save you from path length problems on Windows, but it also speeds up `require` calls (slightly) and even conceals your source code from preying eyes.

It's convenient too. You don't have to change any of your source code. Electron's internal Web APIs from Chromium and the (patched) Node APIs both support reading files from asar archives transparently.

Creating an asar archive

Well, first you need to install the `asar` module globally:

```
npm install -g asar
```

Let's forget about making executables for a second and talk about running your app during development. Let's say your app code is in a `my-app` directory. Run this:

```
asar pack my-app app.asar
```

Now you have created an `app.asar`, which contains your app. Run `electron app.asar` to launch it. That's it.

DISTRIBUTION

Previously, when creating executables, we copied your app source into an `app` directory inside Electron's `Resources` (or `resources`) directory. Instead of that, copy your `app.asar` there (and delete any existing `app` directory in there). You can launch your executable just like you did before. It's that easy to reap the benifits of using an asar archive.

Reading files

Why does this work? Both sets of APIs in Electron support reading files from an asar archive: Web APIs provided by Chromium and Node.js' Node APIs.

WEB APIS

Files inside the archive can be requested from a webpage just like a local file can be (with the `file:` protocol). Here's a renderer process example with jQuery's `$.get`:

```
<script>
const $ = require('jquery');
$.get('package.json', (data) => console.log(data);
</script>
```

This will work even if your app source is in an asar. It'll just work as you're used to. If you have an additional asar next to your `index.html`, you can also reach into that, as asar archives are treated like (virtual) directories and the files in them as normal files in the filesystem.

```
<script>
const $ = require('jquery');
$.get('example.asar/something.txt', (data) =>
console.log(data);
</script>
```

NODE

Node APIs treat asar archives as directories as well, thanks to patches in Electron. See this example using the `fs` module:

```
const fs = require('fs');
fs.readFileSync('/path/to/example.asar/file.txt');
```

How about using a module from inside an asar?

```
require('example.asar/something/blah.js');
```

Exception: reading the asar in its entirety

Since asar archives are treated like directories, you need some extra code if you want to interact with the asar archive like a single file. The `fs` module's patched support for asar archives can be disabled by setting `process.noAsar` to `true`. That's a bit drastic though. Electron was nice enough to allow access to the original unpatched `fs` module as `original-fs`.

```
const originalFs = require('original-fs');
originalFs.readFileSync('example.asar');
```

Downsides

Ok, asar archives aren't completely like directories. They're read-only. So any of your code (or dependencies') code that uses Node APIs to modify files, can't be used with files in an archive.

As the files in an archive aren't really there, `fs.stat` and similar cannot be trusted, except for file size and type.

Since asar archives are treated like virtual directories, there are no actual directories in the filesystem. This means that directories in the asar can't be used as a current working directory (`cwd`) with any Node API.

Unfortunately, some extra overhead of unpacking files from the archive can't be avoided. Some Node APIs rely on passing the real file path to underlying system calls. Electron will extract the needed file into a temporary file and pass the path of the temporary file to the APIs to make them work. The offending methods are:

- `child_process.execFile`
- `child_process.execFileSync`
- `fs.open`
- `fs.openSync`
- `process.dlopen` (which is used by `require` on native modules)

Note: the temporary unpacking of files can trigger false positives with some anti-virus software.

Lastly, there are limitations on executing binary files in an asar archive. You (or a dependency of yours) may normally use `child_process.exec`, `child_process.spawn`, or `child_process.execFile`.

The only method compatible with files in an asar archive is `execFile`. It's really hard for Electron to reliably patch `exec` and `spawn` without side-effects as they accept a command and not a file.

Unpacked files

To workaround some of the problems stated above, you don't have to put all of your files in the archive. When creating your asar archive, you can pass the `--unpack` flag to keep whichever files you like out of the archive.

```
asar pack my-app app.asar --unpack main.js
```

As well as generating an `app.asar`, you will also get an `app.asar.unpacked` directory that contains the unpacked files. When creating your exectuable, you will also need this alongside your `app.asar`.

If you want to see what's in an asar archive, you can run the following:

```
asar list app.asar
```

The better way

So now you know how to manually create executables, but you can do better. You can write some code to automate the creation of executables, but **`electron-packager`**, a module available on npm, makes light work of it. It's pretty much the standard among Electron users. No more copying and pasting stuff around, renaming, rebranding, and more. Plus, it allows you to build apps for other platforms from the one you're currently on. Great!

To install:

```
npm install -g electron-packager
```

Command-line interface

When running in the console, you must give it the following at a minimum:

- Source directory.

- App name.
- The platform(s) you want to build for (`linux`, `win32`, `darwin` (Mac), `all`).
- The architecture you want to build for (`ia32`, `x64`, or `all`).
- Electron version.

For example, running the following would result in two `.exe`s for Windows (32-bit and 64-bit):

```
electron-packager my-app myApp --platform=win32 --arch=all --
version=0.36.7
```

Notice that we said "*for* Windows". You can use `electron-packager` to build on any platform *for* any platform, even all of them at once.It downloads the required Electron binaries (of the given version) for each platform, then goes through the steps we have done previously (manually) for each one.

ADDITIONAL FLAGS

There are a load of optional flags, including `--all`, which is shorthand for `--platform=all --arch=all`. There are platform-specific ones for setting stuff in the Mac `info.plist`, signing for Mac, and so on.

What about asar? Well passing `--asar` will enabling asar archive packaging. Use `--asar-unpack` to specify which files shouldn't be packed into the archive. This accepts a glob; for example:

- `--asar-unpack=*.js`
- `--asar-unpack=path/to/something.txt`

There's a separate `--asar-unpack-dir` flag for directories. This does not accept a glob. Instead you must give the exact path to the directory relative to the source directory: `--asar-unpack-dir=node_modules/something`.

There are a lot of other options, but let's keep it simple as you won't need much more to begin with anyway. To discover the rest, you can check the documentation, run `electron-packager --help`, or you can even use the interactive implementation:

```
npm install -g electron-packager-interactive
```

Once installed, run `electron-packager-interactive` or `epi` to be prompted with each option, step-by-step.

Rebranding

As you can see, it is a lot easier to build for multiple platforms. There's a lot less manual work. The same goes for rebranding, albeit it's still a little awkward. As shown earlier, you provide your app name and the rebranding in that sense is just done for you. The awkward part is changing the icon. There is an `--icon`, but the format required varies per platform. This means that if you want to generate executables for all operating systems at once for example, you'll have to run three separate commands. For Windows, you need an `.ico` (`--icon=something.ico`). For Mac, it's an `.icns` file, and for Linux, well you don't use `--icon` at all. When instantiating your main window, make sure to pass a string to a PNG as the `icon` property. Then that's used in place of `--icon`.

If building for Windows on Mac or Linux, you'll need to have **Wine** installed for this. Otherwise the underlying module (`node-rcedit`) used to edit the `.exe`'s icon will fail.

Programmatic API

Yes, all of this can be done programmatically too. It'll save you from having to type all of those commands and flags each time you want to generate an app. You won't have to remember them either, which is definitely better for teams. You'll need to install `electron-packager` locally for this:

```
npm install --save-dev electron-packager
```

Ok, now let's create a basic script named `build.js`.

```
const electronPackager = require('electron-packager');

var options = {
  dir: './', // current directory is the source directory
  platform: 'darwin',
  arch: 'all',
  name: 'myApp',
  asar: true
};
```

```
electronPackager(options, (error, appPath) => {
  if(error){
    // something went wrong
    throw error;
  }

  console.log('Success! See ' + appPath);
});
```

The above just builds an `.app` for Mac OS X, but the sky is the limit really. All of the optional flags are supported programmatically as well. If you want to test this, create that file at the root of your app source code and run `node build.js`.

You can easily automate building for all three platforms in one script. As well as that, it's not too difficult to tie `electron-packager` into any existing build system you use like Gulp, Grunt, Broccoli, and so on. It's definitely the way to go, because there is one single command for generating all of your executables.

Creating installers

Okay, so we're almost there. We have executables now, but will your users install them? Well, it depends on your potential user base. If they are pretty tech-savvy, then you can get away without having any installers. Instead you can just provide ZIPs for users to download, especially for Mac. An installer isn't as necessary for Mac applications as it is for Windows. It's very acceptable to just provide a ZIP. When Safari downloads a ZIP, it automatically unpacks it. The user can then launch the app from there, in their downloads, or move it wherever they like. This isn't too strange to a Mac user.

There is no real consensus in the Electron community on what to use to make installers. There are actually a whole bunch of different (often target platform exclusive) modules you can use. It isn't simple. You might be tempted not to bother.

This is where **`electron-builder`** comes in. It handles everything, delegating to these tried and tested platform-specific modules when it needs to. When we say everything, we mean everything. `appdmg`, `windows-installer`, and even `electron-packager` are used under the hood. So there's no real reason not to have installers then. Great, because it's simple for end users and is far more professional.

```
npm install --save-dev electron-builder
```

Forget what you know

We do need to throw away our old setup for creating executables because we'll be doing it with `electron-builder` instead. This time, in addition to executables, we'll get installers and more.

Let's take a look at multi-platform builds. You can't create DMGs (the standard way to distribute `.apps`) on any platform for OS X, and it probably won't ever be possible. You also can't sign your `.app` on any other platform. If your app has native dependencies, it can be compiled only on the target platform.

Let's just build on Windows for Windows, on Mac for Mac, and on Linux for Linux. Sure, this will mean three build steps instead of one, but each one of those steps a lot simpler, and you'll have to install fewer dependencies (like Wine) to do tricky cross-platform stuff.

Let's do what we're told

`electron-builder` is pretty opinionated. There are conventions to follow, but that's ok. The developers behind the module know what they're doing. What's good is that a lot of the options and files we'll need to provide will be smartly reused throughout the process.

We'll need a `build` directory at the root of the project to house assets for building the executables and installers. For Windows, you need an `icon.ico` for the app icon. For Mac OS X, an `icon.icns` is required for the app icon and a `background.png` for the DMG background. The `icon.icns` is also required for Linux, because a compatible icon set will be automatically generated from it.

Make sure your `package.json` has `name`, `description`, `version`, and `author` fields. You also need a `build` property, which is where you can stick any options for `electron-packager`:

```
...
"build": {
  "app-bundle-id": "your.id",
  "app-category-type": "your.app.category.type"
}
...
```

So, how do you run the build? Using an npm script, add a `scripts` property to your `package.json` like this:

```
...
"scripts": {
  "pack": "build"
}
...
```

This allows you to run `npm run pack`, which will call `node_modules/.bin/build` (placed there by `electron-builder`). Now check the newly created `dist` directory at the root of your project for your prize.

Note: the script must be named `pack`.

If you need to pass extra options to `electron-packager`, put them in the `build` property in your `package.json`.

Note: there is a programmatic API too. Take a look at the `electron-builder` documentation. You can use it instead of the `build` binary, if for example, you want to tie it into your task runner or build system. The method suggested above is pretty simple, and the programmatic API isn't much different, because it also reads the `build` property from your `package.json`.

Generating the installers

This is pretty simple now. Just add another `dist` script to generate the installers:

```
...
"scripts": {
  "pack": "build",
  "dist": "build"
}
...
```

The `build` binary detects which npm script it was called from and acts accordingly. After running `npm run dist`, the results can be found in the `dist` directory at the root of the project.

Note: If you want to specify the architecture, you can pass an `--arch` flag, with either `ia32` or `x64` as the value. For example:

```
"dist": "build --arch=x64"
```

MAC

We use the term "installer" loosely when it comes to Mac OS X. The closest thing to a Mac installer is a PKG, but the most common way to ship a `.app` is a DMG. Basically, launching a DMG results in a window being shown that encourages the user to move the `.app` to their `Applications` directory.

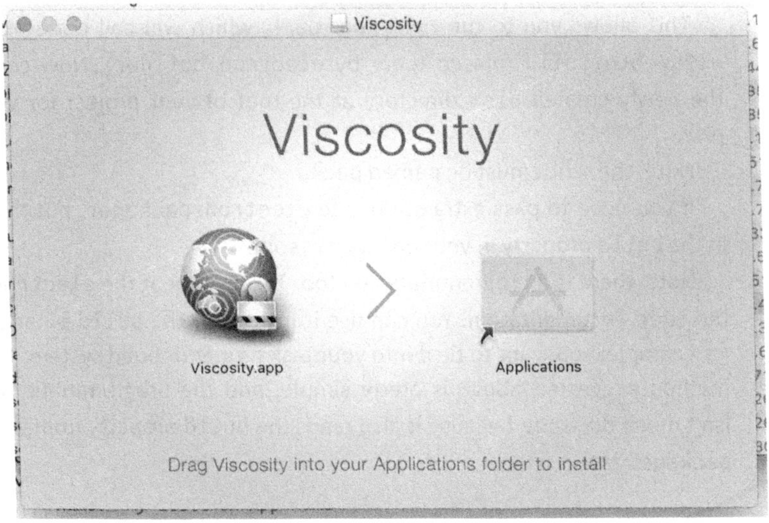

Along with the `background.png` in the `build` directory, the DMG can be customized further by adding an `osx` property under `build`:

```
...
"build": {
  "app-bundle-id": "your.id",
  "app-category-type": "your.app.category.type",
  "osx": {
    "icon-size": 80
  }
}
...
```

You can check out the **appdmg documentation** for more information. Customizing a DMG isn't exactly riveting, so let's move on.

WINDOWS

For Windows installers, `iconUrl` (used for the app icon) is required if you want Windows installers. It must be a HTTP or HTTPS URL, not a local file URL pointing to `build/icon.ico`. Customize the `.exe` installer by putting options for `windows-installer` in a `windows` property.

```
"build": {
  "app-bundle-id": "your.id",
  "app-category-type": "your.app.category.type",
  "iconUrl": "http://something.com/something.ico"
}
```

What's produced is a Squirrel.Windows "installer". This is critical if you want to have automatic updates, but more about that later. Notice how we put "installer" in quotes again. Squirrel.Windows installers are not like your typical installer, since Squirrel.Windows is "Wizard-Free". When a user runs your installer, no dialog shows, but your app just opens. We'll go through this in more detail when we cover automatic updates.

Another noteworthy point is that your app is installed to `%LOCALAPPDATA%\MyApp` (`C:\Users\<username>\AppData\Local\MyApp`) instead of `Program Files` (or `Program Files (x86)`). This is to get around the fact that you need elevated permissions to be able to write, modify, and deletes file in `Program Files`.

If you decide to use another installer, and want to put your app in `Program Files`, or modify files there, don't. If you really really want to, then you'll need those elevated permissions. Your users can run your app as administrator or you can use something like **`node-windows`**. This is a module that allows you to put stuff in the system event log, monitor native Windows services, and run Node.js scripts as Windows services. This gives you an avenue to commands with elevated permissions (with or without the UAC prompt) and more, with interesting methods including `elevate`, `sudo`, and `isAdminUser`. We could spend a chapter going over the abilities `node-windows` unlocks, but we recommend playing it safe and sticking with `AppData`.

LINUX

`electron-builder` just creates executables for Linux. Installers aren't really a thing on Linux. Users know what they're doing and often use a packager manager to install apps (like `apt-get`). As of right now, `electron-builder` only packages your app and creates artifacts for Debian, but RPM support is coming down the line.

Signing

Your apps and executables need to be code-signed. Otherwise, an end user might be blocked from you running it. Use Microsoft SmartScreen, for example. This includes any executables that you bundle into your app (even if it's one of your dependencies), which are spawned at runtime. It also prevents your app from auto-updating, because anti-virus actions might accidentally trigger.

Thankfully, `electron-builder` has recently added the ability to sign as well. For Windows, you need to purchase a signing certificate from any trust certificate authority (like DigiCert). For Mac, you get your certificates through Apple's developer program.

Once you have your certificates, all you need to do is set environment variables and `electron-builder` will take care of the rest. Namely, set CSC_NAME, CSC_LINK and CSC_KEY_PASSWORD. On a development machine, you can get away with just having CSC_NAME. For example, to set CSC_NAME on a Mac:

```
export CSC_NAME="Developer ID Application: My Organization
(ES3F7GPWMK)"
```

Automate everything

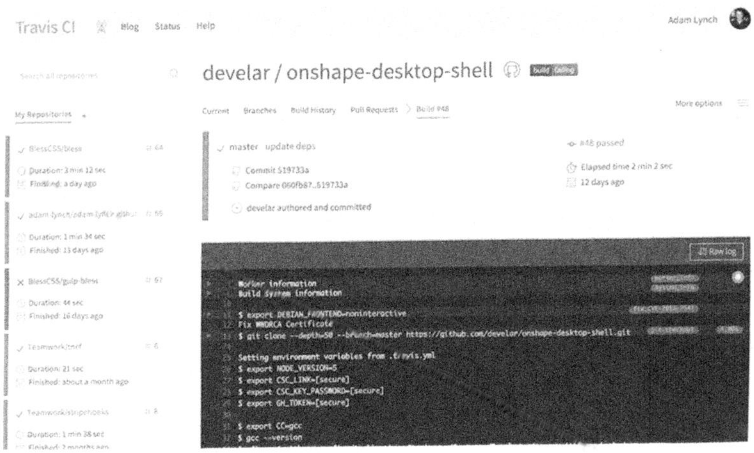

If you want to go all the way with `electron-builder`, there are some handy features and tutorials for using it on continuous integration (CI) and delivery (CD) services, for instance **Travis**, **AppVeyor**, **CodeShip**, and more. These usually support only one platform, such as AppVeyor, which is Windows-only. The idea is that you have a hosted CI server listening to webhooks from GitHub (for example), and once you push a change to your app source, it can run your whole build process for that platform. You can also set up your own CI server with **Jenkins** or similar.

Summary

So there you go, your app is now in users' hands. We've put together executables, branded them, dealt with path length problems, concealed code with asar, and automated the (multi-platform) packaging, first with `electron-packager`, and finally with `electron-builder`. We signed our app to save users from hassle, looked into continuously automating everything, and most importantly, we discovered how to generate installers that actually put our app in a warm cozy place on users' machines. But, what happens if there's a problem with your app after you ship it to your users? What if there's a crash? Well, you can read the *Crash Reporter* chapter if that happens.

You might be have noticed that `electron-builder` created a few extra artifacts. What are these *for*? Well, `electron-builder` covers everything, right? It actually also spits out all the little bits and pieces you need for an auto-updating Electron app, and in the next chapter we will examine automatic updates.

Automatic Updates 12

You don't want to just release your app and leave it at that. You should improve it. You may want to notify all of your users that a new version is released, hoping they will download it and install it themselves. This is awkward and very few people will bother. This isn't viable, but updates can be critical.

In this chapter, we compare a few different approaches to updates, including a few custom approaches, along with using the Mac App Store, as well as Electron's own built-in auto-updater. You'll see how to integrate the updater into your app via client-side hooks and events, as well as figuring out the server side setup for updates. The approach to the server side will vary between platforms, but each are clever in their own right. Some examples are to use a simple protocol, store static files on disk, or even to have no server at all. In the end, we'll come to a compromise and have a server that will cover all of our needs.

So, what traits would an ideal update system have? Well, first of all, it shouldn't require too much from the user. This shouldn't have a lot of steps or take too long from start to finish. We should strive to interrupt the user as little as possible, not waste bandwidth, and never ever ask for a reboot.

This should be integrated as much as possible and feel part of the app. It must be reliable, and the implementation should be as simple as possible. Both the client and server (if any) should be as thin and dumb as possible, while being reasonably flexible. Even though you could technically create your own system, it would be nice if you didn't have to write much code. The fewer manual steps we need to do (as developers) when releasing an update, the better.

Let's take a look at the various ways to update a desktop app.

A standalone updater app

You can have another app that ships with yours, which is always running, with the sole purpose of updating your app. Think Adobe. Sure, there are benefits, like your app can be updated if it's not even running, but you shouldn't do this. Users don't like it, and you don't want to leave a bad taste in their mouths. OK, but you still want to do this? Well then, you need to maintain two apps, and ship them both. You can use Electron and `node-auto-launch` to start your updater on startup, but that is like using a bazooka to hit a fly. Since Electron basically contains Chromium and more, the base app before you add any dependencies or code is way too large. Let's see how to tackle this.

Reinstalling per update

Your app can hit an API or a manifest file hosted somewhere to check for an update, then download the installer for the update, launch it and kill the currently running version. This doesn't tick a lot of boxes on our list of requirements and is too much work for the user.

The Indiana Jones maneuver

Remember the scene from *Indiana Jones and the Raiders of the Lost Ark* where he swipes the golden idol? He's poised to swap it out and put something else in its place. Timing is everything. Well, you could do that with your app, in production.

Let's call the current running app version 1 and the update, version 2.

- Once your running app (version 1) figures out there's a new version available (version 2), it downloads it to a temporary directory.

- When the user decides to install it, version 1 spawns version 2 from the temporary directory. It must pass version 2 some command-line arguments, including the path to version 1, so version 2 knows what its job is (and what phase of the update we're current at).
- Version 1 immediately kills itself.
- Version 2 (running from the temporary directory) launches and either shows a spinner or doesn't show any window at all, leaving the user wondering what's going on.
- Version 2 (running from the temporary directory) copies itself over version 1.
- Version 2 (running from the temporary directory) launches the copy of version 2 now placed in original location, again passing arguments to let it know what phase the update process we're at. Alternatively, localStorage could be used. Although if there's a failure at any point, then the app would always think it's in phase N when it starts.
- Version 2 (running from the temporary directory) immediately kills itself.
- Version 2 starts from the original location.
- Version 2 cleans up the temporary directory.

So every update is completely responsible for every step of the update process at some point in its lifetime on the user's machine. It copies itself over the old version, it is the new version, and it downloads the next update to the temporary directory. All the logic is within the app itself. This conserves bandwidth and the app's interface can easily be updated to reflect what's going on.

The massive downside to this is that, again, the logic is within the app itself. It's also pretty fragile and time sensitive. If you're lucky and there's a fluke failure, then one step fails. Depending on which step fails, the user can then either relaunch the app or reinstall it your app, and it'll be fine to carry on auto-updating when you release more updates. The worst case scenario wouldn't be that hard to achieve though. Where you release an update, users successfully update to it, and then there's a bug in that version preventing it breaking the update system. Trust us, *We know*.

Your users are then stuck on an old version. You must contact each and every user (even the ones who haven't had the problem yet), telling them they must reinstall your app. As well as being disastrous then and there, you'll likely have ignorant users stuck on an old version for a long time. Users might think your app has critical bugs you didn't bother fixing even though you have in later releases.

A lot of NW.js apps update this way.

The heart transplant

If you thought that was convoluted, how about another level of complexity? So there's Electron, and then there's our code. In development, your app (directory) is opened by using a prebuilt Electron binary. Some Electron and NW.js users have looked at this as a way to lighten updates. The idea is to ship your app code separately to the Electron binary, so when there's an update, only your app directory is downloaded and the Electron binary is untouched. This is a bit hacky, but it is possible. Although, any time we've seen this implemented, the update system *only* updates the inner app code, but never the wrapper, and never the binary. That's a bit pointless. At some stage you'll *have* to update the binary. The Electron developers might've fixed a bug and or added a new API or feature. The only way is to make users reinstall your app.

You can build a system in which each update somehow indicates what Electron version it needs, and if the new update does indeed require a newer version, Electron and the inner app are both updated. This is a tricky problem though. That is to ensure you can update the inner app and Electron separately without any problems. Electron isn't under your control, because a "patch" can be released that actually has a breaking change in an API. You could do something stupid. There will always be bugs.

Other problems arise when using this pattern, including Asar related trickiness, but let's not go into it.

This pattern for running your app isn't covered in this book because it's not really advisable. It's more popular among NW.js developers than it is in the Electron community. It's not mentioned in the Electron documentation, and `electron-builder` doesn't support it. Let's move on.

Delta updates

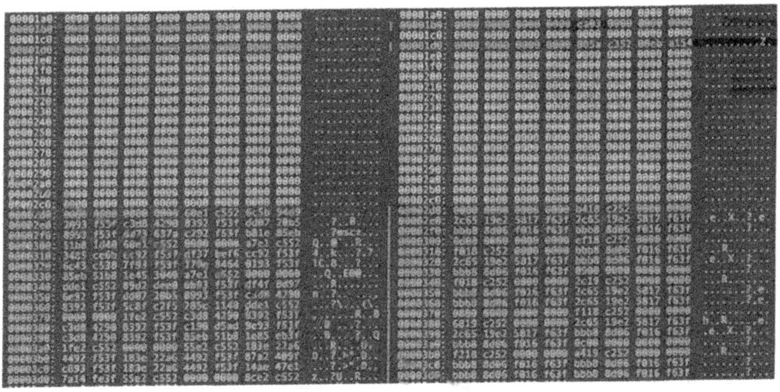

Since we agree we need to update the entire app at once, you can say we're wasting a lot of bandwidth because most of our executable won't be changing. One really cool idea is "delta updates." Somehow somewhere, a "binary diff" is calculated between the current version and the updated version. This diff is downloaded and the old app is patched. Version 1 has evolved into version 2. Updates can be really lightweight in this case, but I actually haven't seen an Electron app yet that does this exclusively.

Electron's autoUpdater

Unlike NW.js, Electron has its own built-in support for auto-updating. First you can only update Mac apps (with support for **Squirrel.Mac**), then **Squirrel.Windows** support was added in version 0.34.1, but there is no support for Linux. You're suggested to use Linux package managers or have downloadable ZIPs instead. You can use one of the methods mentioned above, but it might be a lot of work for one platform.

Electron's system is built on top of the Squirrel framework, which is already used in the wild to update Mac and Windows apps alike. Of course, you can update your apps however you like, but it's great that there's one recommended and reliable way to update your Electron app.

The API is accessible via the `electron` module in your main process:

```
const electron = require('electron');
const autoUpdater = electron.autoUpdater;
```

To initialize the auto-updater, you need to call `autoUpdater.setFeedURL`, giving it a URL that it'll use to check for updates. Note that the URL cannot be changed after this point. Then to check for updates, it's as simple as calling `autoUpdater.checkForUpdates`. This does not accept any arguments; instead of a callback, you must listen for events `autoUpdater` emits:

- `checking-for-update`
- `update-available`
- `update-not-available`
- `update-downloaded`

Once `autoUpdater.checkForUpdates` is called, it'll hit the URL we've given, and if there isn't an update available, the `checking-for-update` then `update-not-available` events will be emitted. If there is an update, `checking-for-update` will be followed by `update-available` and eventually `update-downloaded` once the file is completely downloaded.

`update-downloaded` is the only event that is emitted with some data. The arguments passed to your event listener would be as follows:

- `event` - nothing really interesting here
- `releaseNotes`
- `releaseName`
- `releaseDate`
- `updateURL`

Most of the these arguments can be null or empty, it depends on your server implementation. More about that in awhile.

To actually install the update and restart the app, we have `autoUpdater.quitAndInstall`. This takes no arguments. It's to be called once the `update-download` event has fired and will figure out the rest itself. Within a few seconds, the running app is gone and the update is open in its place.

Here's a more complete yet basic example:

```
const electron = require('electron');
const app = electron.app;
const autoUpdater = electron.autoUpdater;
// ...
```

```
app.on('ready', () => {
    // ...
    // set up window, etc.
    // ...

    autoUpdater.setFeedURL("http://localhost:8989/?
version=0.1.0");

    autoUpdater.on('checking-for-update', () => {
      // ...
    });

    autoUpdater.on('update-available', () => {
      // ...
    });

    autoUpdater.on('update-not-available', () => {
      // ...
    });

    autoUpdater.on('update-downloaded', () => {
      autoUpdater.quitAndInstall();
    });

    // Check right now
    autoUpdater.checkForUpdates();
```

We're not doing anything with most of the events here. These allow you to hook into the update process and tweak your app accordingly. For example: when `update-available` is emitted, you might show a spinner to indicate that an update is being downloaded. We only tell the user there's an update available once it's actually downloaded are ready to go.

Typically, you'd call `checkForUpdates` when the app starts, at a set interval, and when the user clicks a custom button to manually trigger an update check. Of course, all of this must only be done in production (to your packaged app).

It's nice how Electron abstracts all the inner-workings away from us. You'd have no idea that the implementation underneath is actually completely different per platform (Squirrel.Mac versus Squirrel.Windows). Thankfully you don't have to worry about that. Unfortunately, what you need to do on the other side of the equation will vary per platform.

Mac

To use autoUpdater in your Mac app, it must be signed, which is unfortunate if you want to quickly test this. A server is also required for updating your app on a Mac.

When autoUpdater.checkForUpdates is called, a GET request is sent to the URL you gave when initializing autoUpdater. If there isn't an update available, your server must simply respond with a 204 (No Content). If there is an update, it must return a 200 with some JSON.

```
{
    "url": "http://myserver.com/myapp/releases/1.1.0",
    "name": "My Release Name",
    "notes": "Put release notes here, maybe a changelog,
etc.",
    "pub_date": "2016-01-08T18:21:23+01:00"
}
```

Everything is optional except for url. If pub_date exists, it must be formatted according to ISO 8601.

Once your app receives this back from the server, Electron will emit the update-downloaded. Then Electron (or Squirrel.Mac underneath) will request the URL found in url. What's returned must be a ZIP. The request will have an Accept: application/zip header.

As discussed in the last chapter, electron-builder gives you everything you need. Each time you generate a release with npm run dist, a Squirrel.Mac compatible ZIP can be found in the dist directory. At .../dist/my-app-darwin-x64/my-app-mac-1.0.0.zip for example, with 1.0.0 being your app's version in your package.json. This contains the regular complete .app.

Once your app returns the 200, the update will be requested no matter what, even if the version isn't higher, if the app is unchanged, or more. It's completely up to the server to decide whether or not there's an update. That is pretty handy. It might save you in a time of need. You can change the updater logic on the server at any point or even force out updates regardless of versions.

Once the ZIP is downloaded, Electron emits update-downloaded, with the values that were returned back from the first request (pub_date, etc.) being passed as arguments to your callback, which we covered earlier. Now the server is no longer needed, and it's up to you to call autoUpdater.quitAndInstall.

SERVE!

This is pretty simple right? Let's set up a quick example server that always says there's no update available. Create a new directory, run `npm init` to create a `package.json`, and `npm install --save express` to grab ExpressJS. Then stick the following in an `index.js` script:

```
var express = require('express');
var app = express();

app.listen(8989);

app.get('/', (req, res) => {
    res.sendStatus(204);
});
```

So we're creating a server with Express, and listening on port 8989. The server can be started by running `node index.js` (it's best to do this in a new terminal). If you set your `autoUpdater` feed URL to `http://localhost:8989`, then calling `autoUpdater.checkForUpdates` will result in a 204 and therefore `update-unavailable` will be emitted. A (minimalistic) successful example looks like this instead:

```
res.json({url: 'http://localhost:8989/versions/1.1.0'});
```

Since that URL would then be hit, we also need to add that route to express, which responds with the ZIP:

```
const express = require('express');
const fs = require('fs');
const app = express();

app.listen(8989);

app.get('/', (req, res) => {
    res.json({
        url: 'http://localhost:8989/versions/1.1.0'
    });
});

app.get('/versions/1.1.0', (req, res) => {
    fs.readFile('../path/to/dist/my-app-x64/my-app-1.1.0-
mac.zip', (err, data) => {
        if(err){
            console.log(err.message);
```

```
            res.sendStatus(500).json({ error: err.message });
        }

        console.log('Successfully sent back the ZIP');
        res.type('zip');
        res.send(data);
    });
});
```

What we've done here is to use the `fs` module to grab the ZIP and send it back. Obviously, in the real world, you wouldn't have hardcoded routes like this; you'd catch any request to `/versions/*`, parse the version from the route, and so on.

Since the onus is on the server to decide whether or not there's an update available for the user's app, how do we actually know if there is? Well, all requests sent from the user's app will have a `User-Agent` header containing our app's name, version, architecture, and more, such as `my-app/1.0.0 CFNetwork/760.1.2 Darwin/15.0.0 (x86_64)`.

Once we parse out the version number, we need to decide if the version is newer. Let's assume the versions follow Semantic Versioning, which you may remember from the beginning of this book.

Given a version number MAJOR.MINOR.PATCH, increment the:

- MAJOR version when you make incompatible API changes
- MINOR version when you add functionality in a backwards-compatible manner
- PATCH version when you make backwards-compatible bug fixes

Additional labels for pre-release and build metadata are available as extensions to the MAJOR.MINOR.PATCH format.

Since npm itself uses Semantic Versioning to compare module versions, it's no surprise that the code we need is on npm.

```
npm install --save semver
```

Here's our updated example using `semver.gt` to check if the latest update is newer than the app which is checking for updates:

```
var express = require('express');
var semver = require('semver');
var fs = require('fs');
var app = express();
```

```
app.listen(8989);

app.get('/', (req, res) => {
    var version = req.headers['user-agent'].split(/[/ ]/)[1];
    if (semver.gt('1.1.0', version)){
        res.json({
            url: 'http://localhost:8989/versions/1.1.0'
        });
    }
    else {
        res.sendStatus(204);
    }
});

app.get('/versions/1.1.0', (req, res) => {
    fs.readFile('dist/electron-quick-start-darwin-x64/
electron-quick-start-1.1.0-mac.zip', (err, data) => {
        if(err){
            console.log(err.message);
            res.sendStatus(500).json({ error: err.message });
        }

        console.log('Successfully sent back the ZIP');
        res.type('zip');
        res.send(data);
    });
});
```

This code is clearly not production ready but you get the idea. Also, now you know how to test your app's auto-update functionality, locally on your machine.

TAKING IT EVEN FURTHER

As you can see, the requirements for your server are so simple, you can do whatever you want. The ZIPs don't have to be on the server at all, because they can be hosted anywhere. The `url` you return can point directly to the ZIP's URL on AWS S3 for example.

Going even further, since all the logic is on the server, the server can use combinations of determining factors to decide to give the requesting app an update or not. Theoretically, you can add the user's ID to your app's user-agent and then decide whether or not to allow them updates based on their settings, pricing plan, and more.

Windows

To be able to use `autoUpdater` in your Windows app, it has to have been installed with a Squirrel.Windows installer with an application ID, which is what `electron-builder` produces.

As Squirrel.Windows is used, and the under the hood implementation of `autoUpdater` is completely different to the Mac implementation. This is not out of necessity, nor due to some deep rooted Windows awkwardness, but rather by design. The intention is to simply things.

Squirrel.Windows uses NuGet packages to create installation and update packages. As we've covered before, it's "wizard-free." There are no problems with permissons, and you'll never see a UAC (User Account Control) dialog. Checksums are generated and verified to ensure downloads are successful, which is something Squirrel.Mac doesn't do.

It actually updates the app in the background while it's running and the user will see the changes once the app is restarted once we call `autoUpdater.quitAndInstall`. But isn't this only possible on Mac OS X.

It actually supports delta updates as well, which is amazing. So let's say you changed a bit of JavaScript, and the update is just one megabyte in size.

What if the user is a few versions behind? You can't possibly have binary diffs for every possible combination of app versions. So instead, only one delta update is generated per version, from the previous version to the current one. So, if the user is a few versions behind, do we simply have to download the whole new version and perform a full update? Well no, it depends.

Since we have patches from each version to the next, Squirrel.Windows can apply these patches incrementally to the current version the user has, until we eventually end up with the latest version. At a certain point, the overhead is not worth it. When the user is so far behind, a full update becomes the better option, and that's what Squirrel.Windows does.

Best of all, all of this is internal, hidden away from you behind the uniform `autoUpdater` API. We check for updates and install them in the same manner, but underneath, Squirrel.Windows will decide whether to apply a delta updates, multiple, or perform a full update. We can't stress enough how good that is.

Squirrel.Windows was built with support for multiple update channels in mind, just like Google Chrome has production and canary channels. This can be achieved by using slightly different URLs. Although, this isn't technically impossible with Squirrel.Mac either.

You might imagine that with all of that magic and great features, there must be a lot more to the client implementation for the Windows app. There's even more than you think because, unlike Squirrel.Mac, a server is not required.

INSTALLATION

To explain, let's explain what a Squirrel.Windows installer does.

- Ensures the .NET Framework is installed.
- Creates the `%LOCALAPPDATA%\MyApp` directory.
- Extracts an `Update.exe` binary that is built in by `windows-installer` (used by `electron-builder`).
- Extracts `MyApp.1.0.0-full.nupkg` to `%LOCALAPPDATA%\MyApp\packages\temp`.
- Executes `Update.exe`, which copies the full version of your app's files to `MyApp\app-1.0.0` and then launches it.

The first time our app is executed, shortcuts will be created on the desktop and in `AppData`.

WE'LL NEED THAT HEART TRANSPLANT AFTER ALL

The shortcut we discussed earlier as needed for notifications is created by the installer, except it's pretty different. Our app isn't run like you'd expect, since there's a bit of trickery involved. Believe it or not, it's actually run similarly to *The heart transplant* update method I described earlier as a terrible thing to do. Take a look at the shortcut's properties:

- Target: `C:\Users\<username>\AppData\Local\MyApp\Update.exe --processStart MyApp.exe`
- Start in: `C:\Users\<username>\AppData\Local\MyApp\app-1.0.0`

As you can see, when you run your app, it actually calls `Update.exe` with parameters. This makes Squirrel.Windows a go-between. This is a lot lot safer than updating Electron and your own app code separately, as described earlier, though. You can't really break your update system within your app code when using Squirrel.Windows.

THE UPDATE PROCESS

So what does `Update.exe` do?

- Checks for updates. Yes, this logic is on the client-side for Squirrel.Windows.
- Download and verifies the download of update packages.
- Builds the full package from deltas if it needs to.
- Installs the new version (under `app-1.1.0`).
- Updates the shortcuts. Specifically, it changes it to start in the `app-1.1.0` directory, rather than the original `app-1.0.0`. If the shortcut is no longer there, it will put it back.
- Removes old versions. It cleans everything but the current version and the previous version.

As you can see, the shortcut is not a regular shortcut, it changes all the time, and is put recreated on every update if it happens to be removed. So, as you can see, if you're using Squirrel.Windows, it doesn't make sense anymore to create a shortcut programmatically for Windows 8 notifications like we showed you earlier.

WHAT ABOUT THE FILES?

All release artifacts generated from `electron-builder` for Squirrel.Windows need to be hosted somewhere. Just as static files, there's no need for an API. Squirrel.Windows has *a lot* of documentation that includes an example using an AWS S3 bucket for storage, IIS, GitHub releases, and even your local filesystem.

Wait, locally? What? Yes, you can actually store them in a directory on disk and pass the path to the directory to `autoUpdater.checkForUpdates`. This is great for testing automatic updates for app. Apparently, some people even use it when creating a desktop application to run on machines that all have access to a certain network path; think internal company applications.

You *can* have a server, if you want. Check the documentation. There's no real need though.

Common ground

As you can see, if you host your updates somewhere like S3, you can have Squirrel.Windows use it as well as Squirrel.Mac too, albeit with a little server in between.

As you can imagine, `electron-builder`'s additional features for continuously integration services can be fantastic if used to push updates to S3 for every push. You can even use commit IDs in versions.

Mac App Store

What about putting your app in the Mac App Store (MAS)? This would integrate your app more tightly into Mac OS X and the ecosystem. Your app would update via the app store, and you'd have changelogs in the store, and so on. You might want to do this if you want to charge for your app.

You can't actually originally get an Electron app into the MAS; your app would fail the get through the review process as it used some private APIs. Currently, every release of Electron comes with MAS-compatible builds (prefixed with `mas-`). These are changed in certain ways to comply with Apple's MAS rules and restrictions including sandboxing, removing of the `crash-reporter` and `autoUpdater` modules (not a problem since your app updates would be done via the MAS), and more.

To create a Mac App Store build, all you need to do is tweak your `package.json`, and build as normal.

```
...
"build": {
  ...
  "osx": {
    "target": ["mas"]
  },
  ...
},
...
```

Once the `target` property is there, `electron-builder` (and `electron-packager` underneath) will take care of the rest.

Summary

Now that you're informed, you can implement updates however you like. We've covered what makes a good auto-updater. We've taken a look at a few custom options, publishing your app to the Mac App Store (and charging for it), as well as taking a thorough dive into using the `auto-updater` module (for Mac and Windows). As far as the server-side goes, Windows and Mac diverge in interesting ways, but we managed to find a solution that keeps everyone happy. Although, when it comes to Linux, using package managers and or a custom solution is the way to go. Reminder: all code found in this chapter and throughout the book can be found on GitHub at **github.com/adam-lynch/developing-an-electron-edge**.

Crash Reports 13

As soon as you've finished developing your application with Electron, you will get to the point where you're able to ship it to your users. Whether this is via a website or via App Stores, you probably will have a good overview over how many users have downloaded your application. App Stores provide good statistics over who downloaded your application, how many people have uninstalled it since, and users can even use this platform to rate your application and leave comments. However, they provide no information at all about one of the most important things: when the application crashes. Even if you've tested thoroughly on your own machine and probably on different desktop environments, it can still be possible that a user with a different environment comes around and the application crashes on the user's machine. Or another user may find a weird bug that you didn't encounter before, which leads to the application crashing. In all of these cases you probably want to be informed about these crashes.

In this chapter we'll take a look at how you can automatically gather information about application crashes and how to analyze them.

The `crash-reporter` module

Fortunately, Electron ships a `crash-reporter` module that provides the functionality to automatically send crash reports to a certain configured server.

It works like this: the processes in which the crash reporter was started gets monitored by a special process and when they crash, the reporter process then sends specific data about the application, the environment and the crash itself to the server.

You can even add additional custom information that you want to send to the server, which helps identify the cause of the crash.

Usage

On Mac OS X Electron uses the **crashpad** client, which is different from the **breakpad** client that is being used on Windows and Linux. Because of how the `crashpad` client works, you need to initialize the crash reporter for all the processes - main and renderer - for which you want to collect crash reports.

The initialization of the client itself is pretty easy and straightforward:

```
crashReporter.start({
  productName: 'ApplicationName',
  companyName: 'CompanyName',
  submitURL: 'https://server-to-send-crash-reports-to',
  autoSubmit: true,
  extra: {
    additionalInformation: ''
  }
});
```

When your application crashes, the report will now automatically be sent to the specified `submitURL`, and it is being saved on the device itself for further inspections.

Building a crash-reports server

To see what the information that is being sent actually includes, we'll quickly go through the steps that are required to build your own server to receive crash reports.

For that you'll use Node and a fantastic module called **`formidable`**, which enables you to easily parse incoming form data and file uploads.

Please install the package: `npm install --save formidable`

Now let's create `crash-server.js` with the following content:

```
const http = require('http');
const formidable = require('formidable');

const crashServer = http.createServer((req, res) => {
  if (req.url === '/crashes') {
    var form = formidable.IncomingForm();

    form.parse(req, (err, fields, files) => {
      if (err) console.error(err);
```

```
      // right now we just output the information we receive
      console.log(fields);
      console.log(files);
    });
  } else {
    res.end(404);
  }
});

crashServer.listen(1337);
```

Now you just need to create an application that will crash, and send a crash report to your configured server:

```
const electron = require('electron');
const app = electron.app;
const BrowserWindow = electron.BrowserWindow;

const crashReporter = electron.crashReporter;

var mainWindow = null;

app.on('ready', () => {
  crashReporter.start({
    productName: 'AwesomeApp',
    companyName: 'AwesomeCorp',
    submitURL: 'http://localhost:1337/crashes',
    autoSubmit: true,
    extra: {
      name: 'Awesome Electron Application'
    }
  });

  process.crash();
});
```

Now this is some code that you probably wouldn't write in your application (heck, it doesn't even open a renderer process), but you can provoke an actual crash of the application using the `process.crash()` method.

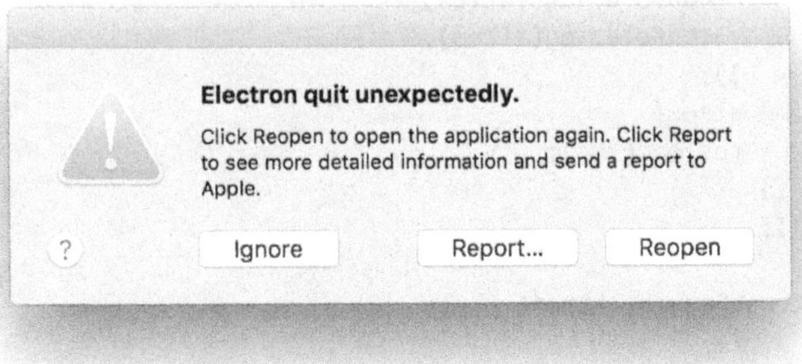

Analyzing the crash report data

Now let's take a look at what we've received in the crash report server:

```
{
  _companyName: 'AwesomeCorp',
  _productName: 'AwesomeApp',
  _version: '0.0.0',
  guid: '9827da34-6457-40b1-9b7f-541cc9bd8413',
  name: 'Awesome Electron Application',
  platform: 'darwin',
  process_type: 'browser',
  prod: 'Electron',
  ver: '0.37.2'
}
```

These are the fields that you receive, including your `extra` information (the specific name set in `main.js`).

We've set the `_productName` and `_companyName` attributes in the options for the crash reporter. The `_version` attribute automatically uses the version of the application set in your `package.json` file. This is very valuable information because you can explicitly see which version was used.

The `guid` attribute is a unique string for the user itself. As long as a user does not uninstall your application, this string stays the same, which makes it easy for you to group those reports by user.

The `platform` attribute shows you which desktop platform the user was on. In our example it shows "`darwin`", because we've run the application on Mac OS X.

The `process_type` attribute is also very important: it shows which process the application did crash. `browser` is from the main process, and `renderer` is from a renderer process.

The `ver` attribute additionally shows you the used Electron version. This could be important to check, in case a specific Electron version has known issues and the user's crash was caused by this.

The `upload_file_minidump` file

You also get the following output from our crash report server:

```
{
  upload_file_minidump: File {
    domain: null,
    _events: {},
    _eventsCount: 0,
    _maxListeners: undefined,
    size: 378496,
    path: '/var/folders/q1/jjvv8fpx2vv0qn6lm2029ph80000gn/T/
upload_d85fc2f38c3ef7b8e73f21ac5c1c094e',
    name: '96fed6e1-3eea-4e32-a8c3-438ed23270d0.dmp',
    type: 'application/octet-stream',
    hash: null,
    lastModifiedDate: Tue Mar 22 2016 18: 29: 58 GMT +
0100(CET),
    _writeStream: WriteStream {
      _writableState: [Object],
      writable: true,
      domain: null,
      _events: {},
      _eventsCount: 0,
      _maxListeners: undefined,
      path: '/var/folders/q1/
jjvv8fpx2vv0qn6lm2029ph80000gn/T/
upload_d85fc2f38c3ef7b8e73f21ac5c1c094e',
      fd: null,
      flags: 'w',
      mode: 438,
      start: undefined,
      pos: undefined,
      bytesWritten: 378496,
      closed: true
```

```
      }
    }
  }
```

This is a file that was attached to the crash report that the `formidable` module automatically parsed and saved in a temporary location. The `name` attribute shows the original filename.

The `.dmp` extension may look a bit strange to you. It is actually a dump file that was automatically generated by the `crashpad` (if you're on Mac OS X) or the `breakpad` (Linux and Windows platforms) client. The format is called `minidump`, and it is the same one that the Windows platform uses for it's own crash reports.

Analyzing those dumps can be pretty complicated, and the Chromium Developers wiki has it's **own page dedicated** on that topic.

Opening the file is currently only possible on the Windows platforms. Visual Studio, which is also available in a free version, knows the file type and can open dump files.

If you open the generated dump file in Vistual studio, it shows a summary of the dump, system information, and the loaded modules.

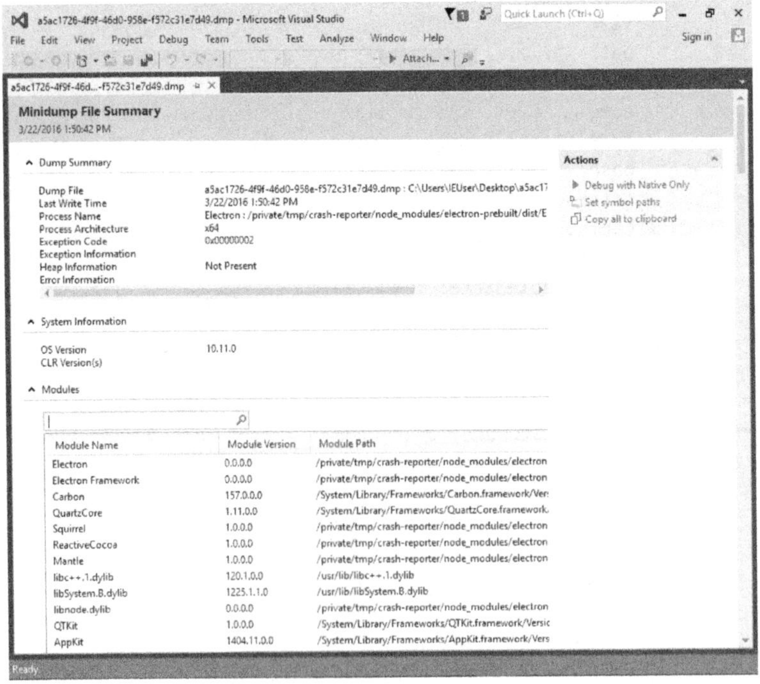

Unfortunately, it can't give you an exact stack trace of where in a file the error happened, but it does show you the modules that were loaded while the application crashed. As you can see, that dump is only partly valuable to us.

As you've now seen, crash reports can be very valuable, however, analyzing crash dumps can be a huge pain. If you don't want to get knees-deep into the details of the crash dump, you can just try to reproduce those reported crashes under the exact same environment that the user has. Most of the time the reason for those crashes can be found either in Electron's known issues for the used version, or maybe for a Native Addon that you're using that may not run under all three desktop environments.

The crash-reports server that we've written can obviously be improved a lot, for example by sending the data as email. But this is up to you! This should be enough to just get you started using crash reports in your Electron application.

Summary

Now that you've made it all the way through the book, we believe you're ready to build all sorts of wonderful applications! With Electron, developing native applications is not only easy, it's also very powerful because these applications run on all desktop platforms. Also, between the whole Node.js ecosystem and npm, you have access to hundreds of thousands of great packages written by the community. The number of people who use GitHub's Atom every day has surpassed one million, and along with it, desktop app development has improved by leaps and bounds. The future looks bright.

Who knows, maybe we'll run into you on Github or in an Electron chatroom. Please make sure to let us know when you've built a real application after reading this book!

Made in the USA
Monee, IL
05 November 2026

67845303R00115